AGENTS OF EVOLUTION

To our evolution!

M

NEW DEGREE PRESS

AGENTS OF EVOLUTION
An Astrological Guide For Transformative Times

ISBN   978-1-63676-889-2   Paperback
        978-1-63676-890-8   Kindle Ebook
        978-1-63676-891-5   Ebook

AGENTS
OF
EVOLUTION

AN ASTROLOGICAL GUIDE
FOR TRANSFORMATIVE TIMES

MARGA CHEMPOLIL LAUBE

Dedicated to you, dear reader.

Fathoms

Is the sea to me,
the nature of Nature

Is not jail

Is almost June now
and twice as opulent
in my kitchen of kitchens,
water kettle always over the flame
for when you arrive

How we will explode
the library
like a summer dandelion

Is water, our body.
Fathoms of
jubilated rain

Is not death

Is my owl, and yours
stringing night-times
awake,
over the multi-colored sky

Is the form of Rain,
my name for you

the slosh of your voyage
beginning

CONTENTS

PREFACE

——

I heard the crack and instantly knew something was wrong. I didn't want to look at it, knowing I would probably faint at the sight of the mangled form. It was March 31, 2020, and lockdown was about to begin in the little Oregon mountain valley where I live. Not a great time to break a wrist.

I had pulled open that trap door with its rope pulley system every day for months without incident. But finally, that morning, the frayed rope had snapped, and I went flying, fracturing a joint I could not afford to do without for any length of time—especially not during a pandemic lockdown, when self-sufficiency would be essential.

Any of the global problems we face may erupt like that. We sense there's something we need to address to prevent calamities from sneaking up on us and unleashing a world of hurt at super inconvenient times. It rumbles and titters in the background of our thoughts, the distinct possibility that we could be on the brink of human extinction. That is what is at stake. Deep in our bones, I think we all know it.

I got myself downstairs to my kitchen and laid on the floor, dizzy, losing consciousness. Semi-lucid, I called my sister and asked her to drive me to the hospital. The next six months were hard. Maybe if I had gotten the rope repaired when I first noticed it was frayed, I could have spared myself the trouble. . .

The world's leading scientists have been issuing compelling warnings for over thirty years about the collision course humanity is on with the natural world. (Elgin, 2020) As recently as February 2021, over five hundred scientists and scholars from over thirty countries signed their names to a "Scholars Warning" on the risks of societal disruption and collapse as a result of climate crisis, published in a letter to *The Guardian*. Why are we not acknowledging and putting all of our collective resources toward addressing the problems the world's brightest are warning us about?

THE WRITING ON THE WALL

We're a hot mess. It's as if Earth's body politic has a collective fever. A growing cluster of crises is gaining magnitude, spreading rapidly over the Earth. We see the signs in our water systems, food systems, ecosystems, in the public health of populations, in governments, in the world economy, and in the political polarization playing out on the world stage.

Those same signs are reflected in the astrology of the times. Leading up to 2020, most astrologers, including me, saw the conjunction of Jupiter, Saturn, and Pluto as a sign of societal disruption. I did not know that alignment would take the shape of a pandemic, but it told me what 2020 would *feel* like. I knew its energy signature. This is how I attempted to describe what I was sensing to clients: "collectively transformative; the end of one epoch and the beginning of another; death and rebirth of existing systems; a reset; an overhaul of governing ideologies."

When confronted with stark realities such as climate crisis, world hunger, systemic racism, and economic disparity among the world's peoples, most of us are not heartless and uncaring. It's more that we go numb thinking about such big problems and justify the numbness by kidding ourselves into believing some big entity with lots of money and authority is on it (and therefore, we don't have to be). I am no exception.

It took thirty-two years to fully admit to myself that I am an astrologer. I was not excited to come back to my astrological practice after taking a multiple-year sabbatical to work in film. Given the way our general culture views astrology as a pseudoscience and the way it invalidates astrologers, film felt like a more friendly place to be. Yet, I knew I had to come back to astrological practice. I had been given the training to read the movements in the heavens and could not ignore the highly transformative astrological weather patterns I was seeing. I felt a responsibility to come back and report on those patterns, on my growing awareness about the tie-in between personal and collective evolution, and how utterly critical each person's own development is to survival of the human race.

Our human evolution is collective.

Because our human evolution is collective, none of us actually individually evolve until real change is made to prevailing systems that cause harm. We simply pass the hard work of evolution down to the next generations.

I urge you not to do that. Be a good ancestor. Do your work now so the next generations have a chance at a good life.

Evolution is the development of our capacity to embody, both individually and collectively, the truth of who we are.

The reason I wrote this book is because I know reaching critical mass on addressing the meta crisis that lies before us depends on people like you and me becoming galvanized to live at our evolutionary edge. Living quiet, decent lives is not enough right now. You have more in you than that. Governments, big business, non-governmental organizations (NGOs)—none of them can take us in a good direction if you and I are not aware of the impact we have on our world. We are much more significant than we think. We are the ones who make up those governments, businesses, and NGOs. We are the ones we have been waiting for. By staying at our evolutionary edge, *you and I* will bring about solutions to our collective problems.

WHO IS AN AGENT OF EVOLUTION?

You would not have been drawn to opening this book if you weren't an Agent of Evolution. The intention of this book is to catalyze your evolution. I possess no magic powers to do this. Your growth will quicken if you choose to engage with the evolutionary concepts presented and accept my invitation to stay at your evolutionary edge.

In order to benefit from this book, you will need to apply yourself to the material, see yourself in the stories, and mull over the concepts presented. You probably will not agree with everything I say. However, you don't need to in order to gain from this book. Test the concepts presented in your own mind, take what is useful, and discard what isn't. Your evolutionary journey will be completely unique to you. Treat this book like a compass—a navigational guide that can help you align with the direction pointing toward your deepest truth.

HOW THE STARS UNITE US

"Ours is an age between worldviews, creative yet disoriented, a transitional era when the old cultural vision no longer holds and the new has not yet constellated. Yet, we are not without signs of what the new might look like."

—RICHARD TARNAS, COSMOS AND PSYCHE

In order to trust the navigational tools I am presenting, you will want to approach astrology with openness. Please indulge me while I share some insights about astrology you may want to understand before we begin.

I came to the study of astrology in my late teens, living in New York City, hoping it would help me find my way through life. Now in my fifties, I wake up tuning into where the moon and the planets are in the sky, and like a person who always knows where East lies, my inner compass is entirely rooted in this universal, mystical-astronomical context.

As a study of time cycles, astrology can help us understand our place in the whole scheme of Life. Astrology has been used by people for at least five thousand years to organize themselves, plan harvests, prepare for lean times, solve conflicts, and develop spiritually. (Campion, 2008)

More and more, astrology shows me how everything is connected. It elegantly mirrors the central, core principle of many of the world's great spiritualities: we are One. Not just one world, but one organism. We are one massive, complex system of interdependent pieces. Each of us *is* the collective—fractals in the vast cosmic galaxy. Thus, Life evolves *as one* system.

When something happens for a single human being, it can have far-reaching effects for the whole system. We evolve both individually and collectively, in mind-bendingly interdependent ways. Your individual evolution speeds up mine. When the collective is ready to evolve certain aspects of its own awareness, you have more evolutionary juice available to you—more than you may have ever realized before.

CAMPFIRE LESSONS ON COLLECTIVE ASTROLOGY

The October, pre-dawn sky revealed Jupiter sandwiched against the backdrop of the constellation of the Virgin, with Mars and Venus close by. Any astrologer trained in the basics would be able to tell you this happened in the year 2004 of the Gregorian calendar. I was deep in the High Sierras with my Vedic Astrology teacher, James Kelleher, and a small group of other backpackers. My training as an astrologer did not come in the form of book study alone. It involved studying life, intimately. To me, there is nothing more intimate than an October sky as seen from ten thousand feet up a mountainside in the American West.

I asked James whether Jyotish, or Vedic Astrology, could teach us anything about our collective evolution. Until that point, I had been studying the principles of individual chart interpretation.

"Astrology helps us individuals understand and give some meaning to the period we're in," James began. "And it can also do that on a global, geopolitical level. Just as karma *ripens for individuals, it also ripens for groups of people."*

I was about to receive one of my first lessons in "mundane astrology," also called political astrology, which is when you examine the chart of a country or a political leader for collective patterns pertaining to that nation. Learning that way, around a campfire under the stars, makes astrology come alive like no classroom situation ever could. For one thing, it helps you see how small you are in this vast, intricate, interconnected universe; it helps right-size you. It also helps to put you in direct relationship with what you are studying in a way that abstract, cerebral approaches cannot. And it helps seal the learning into your whole being—not just your mind, but also your body and heart.

In the year 2020, my beautiful memory of that trip in the wilderness inspired me to pick up the phone and ask James some more questions. The relationship between a *jyotishi* and their student is a lifetime sort of thing. You don't take a set of classes, go for a certification, and call it good. All sorts of personal development are lightly overseen by your mentor, as part of a lifelong training.

As always, James had a way of clarifying techniques that made sense to me. "It's hard to look at everybody's chart in a country, but you can look at small groups of people," he explained. "You can look at the Kennedy family and see the collective karma, where each one of the members of the family will reflect the karma of losing certain members of that family."

Yikes. The implications were enormous.

"So it happens in all kinds of groups—families, cities, countries. The time when karma will ripen can be seen in the charts of countries, sometimes by looking at the chart of the country, or at the chart of the leader of the country." I was all ears.

It is James Kelleher's *rectification* of the United States' chart that is popularly used with Vedic Astrologers in the US. That chart is set for the signing of the Declaration of Independence, at 6:30 p.m., July 4, 1776, Philadelphia, Pennsylvania. He spent months sifting through historical data to present that chart to the astrological community.

"Collective karma is something you can look at, and the symbols of astrology help you gain insight and understanding about what's going on," he explains. "You look at its symbol and it helps you step outside your own subjective experience, which helps you to stop projecting what you think, or hope, might be. It helps you stop telling yourself a story about it. It helps you gain clarity."

LOTS OF RIPE KARMA

At the 2010 World Conference on Mundane Astrology, one of James's own Jyotish teachers, Swami Sivanandamurthy, predicted that in 2020, chaos and unhappiness would reign and *dharma* would be at its lowest point (implying world crisis), with abundance, support, and peace of mind being harder to access in general.

With Swami Sivanandamurthy's guidance and encouragement, James began researching the astrological influences around 2020 and made a stunning prediction of a worldwide pandemic in January 2020 in his annual 2016 World Predictions presentation. (Kelleher, 2016)

"And the rest is history."

With the many interconnected global crises on earth—pandemics, climate crisis, world population, racial injustice, the gross inequities between the uber-wealthy and the poor—we humans have a lot of ripe karma on our collective plate.

The world has seen times of massive uncertainty before, when earth's inhabitants weren't doing so well and where everything seemed like it might collapse. Imagine living through the first half of the twentieth century, when the world experienced its first World War, the detonation of the first atomic bombs, and the Great Depression. Astrology has been with us humans through all of those times, silently guiding those willing to take in its wisdom.

This time, though, the stakes are higher. In his book *Choosing Earth*, Duane Elgin explains why today's meta crisis is different: "Although human societies have confronted major hurdles throughout history, the challenges of our era are unique in one crucial respect: most are planetary in scope... Never before has humanity confronted a crisis that is devastating the entire biosphere and crippling the ecological foundations for all life." Though there is no guarantee we will make it through this set of crises, and though astrology cannot save the day, it can function as a beacon in difficult times.

WHAT ASTROLOGY IS AND IS NOT

Astrology does not have a great batting average when it comes to pinpointing what exact event will transpire. Astrology also cannot tell us what to do in response to what happens, and it certainly will not do it for us—we must make the choices ourselves. Yet, astrology is amazingly effective at pointing to, in archetypal story form, what *energies* we might experience and when. (By energies, I mean the inner sensations, movements, emotions, and thought processes that can accompany the growth opportunities inherent in every outer event.)

Of course, the realm of archetypal story is not quite the same as fact; as long as factual certainty is not the expectation you are coming to astrology with, you stand to gain. The parallels exist, but that does not mean we can derive nice, tidy equations from them to come up with precise answers to the world's problems. With search engines at our fingertips, our impatience with our human story continually increases, encouraging us to expect instant answers to all our questions. Yet deep down we know that as the hero in our own story, we need to wrestle with the awareness the story produces, what the story teaches us, live with it for a spell, and let it shape us. Archetypal story provides no download of facts pointing the way forward; it requires our active participation.

Story is its own kind of language, less a jagged, angular precision and more a round, tumbling flow. Music is another language in this same non-rational, more right-brained domain. It is possible to convey things through music that cannot be conveyed through words. We can all sense this as self-evident.

Though astrology also uses data and pattern analysis to *determine* future trends, astrology *communicates* more like music than like stock market analysis.

ASTROLOGY IS A LANGUAGE

At its best, astrology as it is practiced today is a living language. It can communicate nuance and dimensions that scientific, left-brain, factually dominated thinking cannot.

It takes an entire community of astrologers to painstakingly observe, over generations, the effects of an unknown element (like a newly identified asteroid, for instance), agree with one another on significations, and develop a way of using language to translate what we have observed. (This has been done largely without the benefit of publicly funded research— the research has continued, in private, due to generations of dedicated astrologers.) In this way, astrology develops more like a language art than a science. In the same way that words are added to the lexicon of a language based on their popular usage, meanings assigned to the movements of our solar system come about through observation and agreement within the astrological community. These agreements are not always easily reached. We astrologers have heated debates and disagreements, just as I imagine the folks at Merriam-Webster do.

Similar to story and music, astrology communicates in its own way, morphing and changing to reflect the humans who speak it. Do you believe in fables? Do you believe in the mirror? Those are somewhat non-sensical questions, aren't they? Fables and reflections don't belong in the realm of "belief."

Neither does astrology.

ASTROLOGY IS A REFLECTION OF OUR HUMAN EXPERIENCE

Carl Jung, the founder of analytical psychology, said astrology represents "the sum of all the psychological knowledge of antiquity." Countering the often-laid criticism of astrology that there is no demonstrable cause-effect relationship between planets and stars and the lives of humans, he offered up his notion of "synchronicity," which observes that events—such as between human events and planetary movements—can be meaningfully related even when there is no cause and effect relationship.

In his book *Jung on Astrology*, professor and author Keiron Le Grice explains an important facet of Jung's concept of synchronicity: "Jung introduces this idea of what he calls an 'a-causal, general orderedness,' saying that synchronicity is an expression of this underlying principle of order that seems to run through reality." Le Grice further clarifies that order is connected to what Jung calls "a 'transcendental, psycho-physical background' to reality."

On that note, whether or not astrology is "real" seems, almost literally, beside the point. Astrology may be more accurately a concurrent reality or order, capable of giving us reflection on our human development in a way somewhat similar to how mercury in a thermometer can tell us something about temperature.

What did it take for humans to believe the mercury in a thermometer could help them know how to dress when they left their houses? Probably a bunch of really cold days when it was mission-critical to know whether it was going to freeze or not. Do you struggle with your belief in the thermometer? No, of course not—you just use the damn thing!

Similarly, it might take global crises like the ones we're seeing presently for humans to finally decide that astrology might be worth paying attention to.

ASTROLOGY IS SOUL ECOLOGY

As an astrologer, I have been trained (and continue to learn) how to read the natural world. This mystical relationship with the natural world is at the basis of all astrological wisdom and insight. The stars are, after all, part of the natural world—only instead of studying, say, the patterns of lichen on bark in a rainforest, I study the patterns made by celestial orbs in our solar system visible to us as specks of light in the sky. I too am concerned with a kind of ecology, just of a different order.

Rather than relying on scientific reason to prove hypotheses, I use a more direct observation, one that is not unlike an animist's communication with the natural world around her.

Animist, author, and educator Dr. Daniel Foor tells us, "Animists see the world as full of persons, both human and other-than-human, and prioritize living in conscious and respectful ways with others. These others include: animals, plants, mountains, metals, fire, bodies of water, spirits of wind and weather, deities, ancestors, star people, nature spirits, and many others."

Nature speaks with us all the time, every minute of every day. The drama of a windstorm that wakes you up in the middle of the night might speak of changes coming. A gentle rain falling as you are going to sleep might bring comfort and relaxation and, in turn, a knowledge that all will be well. The calls of an owl heard faintly in the distance might be warning of a loss soon to take place. None of these communications from nature can be codified into hard and fast if/then statements. They must be interpreted in the context of the ongoing, living relationships they are a part of, along with countless co-arising vectors of physical experience, not through our minds but through our animal bodies.

Have you ever watched a hawk riding thermals? What arose inside your own body as you witnessed their relaxed grace? Animals have a natural world intelligence that we can learn from.

Author of *Becoming Animal*, David Abram puts it this way:

> *Never having separated their sentience from their sensate bodies. . . many undomesticated animals, when awake, move in a fairly constant dialogue not with themselves but with their surroundings. Here it is not an isolated*

mind but rather the sensate, muscled body itself that is doing the thinking, its diverse senses and its flexing limbs playing off one another as it feels out fresh solutions to problems posed, adjusting old habits (and ancestral patterns) to present circumstances.

I believe we cut ourselves off from a profound source of wisdom when we stop trusting the depth of knowing produced by the "sensate, muscled body." We *are* animals. The fact that we have pre-frontal cortexes is no reason to trivialize the other, more ancient mammalian and reptilian ways of knowing the world around us and our place in it.

The same is true for knowing what the stars are telling us.

ASTROLOGY IS A GATEWAY PRACTICE

Astrology is sort of a "gateway practice" for us lost Westerners who do not yet remember our place in the natural order of things. Astrology still allows us to use our minds to make sense and meaning of the natural world around us. Astrology can function as training wheels, helping us return to a higher order of direct "knowing" that the Western world abandoned sometime around the seventeenth century when scientific reason had us divide the disciplines of astronomy and astrology. (O'Hara, 2021)

As you explore the pages of this book, perhaps hold lightly that your relationship to the planets and stars is not as distant as you think. Much like we might attempt to know our way around a given environment on Earth by visiting it, noticing things about it, recording what we see, so too can we develop a relationship with our solar system.

In the same way that poetry helps us know ineffable things about our lives that rational thought can't quite get to, astrology helps us access some of that more direct animal knowing about our lives that pros and cons lists can't touch.

THROUGH THE LENS OF ASTROLOGY

Today it is commonly accepted wisdom that we cannot solve problems with the same level of thinking that created them. Many of us intuitively sense that the solutions to our global problems lie somewhere outside the frameworks we are already considering.

Today, top authorities are not seriously consulting astrology to understand our global crises—not publicly, at least. But what if astrology was exactly that new framework needed to provide critical, game-changing, collective self-reflection on our global problems?

One of the founders of Evolutionary Astrology, Steven Forrest, writes in his book *The Inner Sky*, "Astrology is just one more path to self-knowledge. [Its] principal advantage is speed."

Forrest goes on to say, "Without [astrology], we may stumble around for years trying to sort out good information about who we are from all the phony truths and empty dreams with which we have been programmed. Psychotherapy may accelerate the process. So might a dynamic marriage. So might an adventure that pushes us to the limits of endurance, stripping away everything but the barest essentials of our character. But all those processes take time."

What astrology lacks in predictive accuracy, it more than makes up for in its ability to raise the mirror of self-recognition, *in record time.*

In my astrology practice, people often first come to me in crisis, at a moment when they have received their own personal evolutionary call, only when all else has failed to help them. I propose that the meta crisis we are facing as a human species is our *collective* evolutionary call. Will we hear the call as the evolutionary opportunity it is? In responding to that call, will we allow more ancient ways of knowing, like astrology, to guide us forward?

This book provides you with the astrological contemplations necessary to awaken your own personal response to our collective evolutionary call.

INTRODUCTION

———

I am standing on the balcony of the San Francisco Art Institute on a crisp September day in 2019. As I take in the sweeping vistas of the bay, dwellings precariously stacked on the hillsides like so many delicate, brightly colored blocks piled high in a bold, metropolitan flourish come into view. Tomorrow, I will be filming at the Global Climate Strike organized by youth for a documentary I am working on about climate crisis. A palpable frenzy permeates the social air. My phone is blowing up with texts about how great the strike is going to be and posts about Greta Thunberg, the human icon for this political moment.

But I feel a deeper pulse below the surface of our jittery enthusiasm. It moves as a gray blob surrounding the whole land mass of the San Francisco Bay Area. It deals in dread and fear, and it is buttoned up in a stylish costume of denial. My astrologer self knows that next year, in 2020, a historic conjunction of the planets Jupiter, Saturn, and Pluto promises a grand shake-up of our social structures. I think it's likely to be massive climate events. All the protests, all the films, all the Band-Aid-like positive actions in the world won't amount to a hill of beans when a climate event hits this area. I pause as my stomach sinks beneath me, standing on this balcony in the Russian Hill district, attempting to feel my feet on solid ground.

Aware of my privilege to be in San Francisco on this balcony right now, memories from my twenties, my thirties, my forties, and now my fifties return to me. I took up residence in many of her neighborhoods from 1997 to 2000 and have returned since then for months at a time for stints of work. Her hills live in my bones. Her waters run in my blood. Her stories have put the contours in my language. This city, more lover than zip code, more muse than metropolis, has called and shaped and grown my artistic Soul in inexpressible ways.

Like many of us, at some point in my early thirties, a little after my Saturn Return, I realized I would not be able to walk the traditional path of career and family as defined by my culture. My awareness had me probing into what makes us human beings who we are and how to understand our place in the grand scheme of things. I went on to pursue spiritual paths, healing modalities, and ancient wisdom teachings that offered me clues into these vast subjects. For many years I tried to keep up the facade of being "normal," holding down jobs and continuing with lines of work that would help me fit in, even trying on marriage a couple of times. But more and more, the Path itself led me toward a very unique life—one that exquisitely expressed my true colors. San Francisco had been able to meet me through all those stages of metamorphosis. And here she lay, chugging and heaving before me.

Intimacy with San Francisco as muse allowed me a style of animistic communication with her, familiar to indigenous peoples.

I found I could speak with her, seek her counsel, relate to her, much like I would relate to a beloved person. She is a being, after all. Just because she's not human doesn't mean she doesn't hear me and, when I'm lucky, answer me back.

Standing on that balcony with the wind whipping at the waters not far below, I asked her if she would inevitably succumb to the entropy of climate disasters, political decay, economic breakdown, and social collapse. Protests won't prevent your demise from happening, I thoughtfully lamented to her, my beloved San Francisco, now glinting like a many-faceted jewel in the mid-day sun. Neither will films. Nor big movements throwing good intentions at the growing problems.

She seemed to receive this confession of my deepest fears, the wind picking up in response. I grew quiet, leaning into the pause in our conversation. Then, randomly reflecting on all the people I would be meeting the next day, all the kind, caring, excellent, bright beings all doing the best we knew how, I presented these images to her, and she shot right back, a small leaf landing at my feet.

"Start where you are," the leaf seemed to say as it blew my way.

"Oh, that's realistic," I was now muttering out loud to myself. "What can any one person do in the face of possible human extinction? These problems are bigger than I am."

The beauty and movement of her mists offered comfort to that weak-kneed part of me losing courage: You are not one person. You are multitudes. Through me, you are connected. Together, you are vast. *I could feel in my body that I was not alone. And so, I began tuning in to these others all feeling these same feels, growing these same antennae, sending and receiving signals from points all along the Earth.*

THE MAGICAL SYMPHONY ASTROLOGERS ARE PRIVILEGED TO HEAR

My work reading thousands of astrological birth charts and counseling both individuals and groups over nearly thirty years has helped me see that the Earth and all her inhabitants are one vast organism made up of interdependent systems.

Witnessing how when one client in some corner of the globe finally makes an evolutionary leap, a whole chorus of others echo those same developments. . . this is the magical symphony astrologers are privileged to hear.

This is what I would like to describe to you in these pages— how together, doing our individual evolutionary "work," we create solutions to our collective problems.

One result of viewing our lives as interdependent is that when I work with a client, I believe them. I see the inherent brilliance in however it is they show up in the world. Rather than pathologize their choices or behaviors, I focus on what they are doing right, knowing they are listening to their inner conductor. Their ability to follow that conductor's cues is pivotal to our collective well-being. In reading their astrological chart, my hope is that I will be able to give them clues about their lives that help them play their part impeccably. I don't see any of the planets or signs as inherently bad or problematic. I look for the contribution that each sound makes within the symphony.

The best way for me to let you hear a little of the symphony is to invite you on a guided tour through our night sky.

A TOUR THROUGH OUR SOLAR SYSTEM

Consider me your tour guide through our solar system. Right now, we are standing at basecamp Planet Earth while I give you a little context for the voyage on which we are about to embark. I hope you brought your hats and sunscreen.

In the coming chapters, I will be taking you on nine major planetary pilgrimages within our solar system: the Sun, the Moon, Mercury, Venus, Mars, Jupiter, Saturn, Rahu, and Ketu. (Those last two are not actual celestial bodies but astrologically significant, mathematically derived points related to eclipses.)

During each of these planetary pilgrimages, I will describe the astrological meaning of that planet, spinning narratives you can relate to within your own life. I will tell personal stories to serve as examples of that planet's energy. I will unpack for you what that particular planet's evolutionary path entails and give examples of other Agents of Evolution who are walking that path. I will offer some mementos you can bring home with you—writing prompts and practices that serve as reminders of what you experienced during your pilgrimage to that planet.

Before we head out, we need to cover a few contextual points that I hope will enhance your experience of the voyage.

A WORD ABOUT THE MAHATMAS FEATURED IN THESE PAGES

The word *mahatma* means "great Soul," or "great being." While many of the scholars featured at each of the planetary reflection sites are men, the mahatmas featured as *Agents of Evolution* are all women, and most are women of color. There are plenty of male mahatmas, but in this book, I chose to feature women, and primarily women of color, to offer representation and elevation to those stories which are more often overlooked.

The Agents of Evolution I feature are activists whose stories I aim to elevate across diverse communities. Their lives are mostly public ones. This does not mean everyone walking an evolutionary path needs to become an activist or even an extrovert. It is simply more effective to demonstrate a principle with someone whose actions have public visibility.

As a living language, astrology sounds different on the tongue of each person who speaks it. Once a practitioner learns basic astrological principles, it is up to them how to interpret those principles. Each astrologer will have their own interpretations of the evolutionary requirements presented by the movements of the planets. Therefore, this book lays no claim to representing all astrologers. The stories presented here are stories I feel move in the direction the evolutionary arrow is pointing.

A WORD ABOUT ASTROLOGY APPRECIATION

Though we tour the astrological planets, this book will not teach you the system of astrology. (For some recommendations on learning astrology itself, please reference the resources section in the back of this book.)

In the way that a music appreciation class delves into aspects of music teaching you how to *hear* music but not necessarily how to *play* music, this book will delve deeply into one of astrology's primary topics—the planets—so that these astrological insights can inform your own evolutionary journey. You will be learning how to *perceive* the astrological planets in your own life, but you will not be learning how to read charts.

Just like not knowing how to play music does not limit your ability to appreciate music, not knowing astrology has no bearing on deriving usefulness from this book. The principles presented are broad enough to benefit everyone. This book aims to give you a *feeling* for each of the planets and show how you can work with that particular energy for your own evolution.

If you work with an astrologer, ask them which of the planets covered in this book is strong in your chart and pay special attention to that chapter. The chapter of your strongest planet is likely to lay out a breadcrumb trail for your most dynamic evolutionary pathway.

As you read, notice which planets speak to you. Most of us have stronger affinities with certain planets and less awareness of and facility with others. Paying particular attention to the chapters of planets you *don't* feel a strong resonance with will help you cultivate balance in your life.

As an astrological guide, this book can help point you to your own true north. When a certain piece of material makes your heart sing, dwell there. Walk *that* path.

A WORD ABOUT THE FOCUS ON PLANETS IN THIS BOOK

"May the Earth and atmospheric powers be peaceful to us.
May the planets that move in Heaven (divicarā grahāh) give
us peace.
May the planets (grahāh) and the Moon give us peace.
May the Sun and Rahu give us peace."

—ATHARVA VEDA XIX.6.7, 10

Most astrological interpretation revolves around three cornerstones: planets, signs, and houses.

If human experience were a sentence, the planets would be nouns, the signs would be verbs, and the houses would be direct objects.

The planets are the main characters in the human narrative. The ancient seers, the sages or *rishis* of India, observed the planets' movements and noticed how our human lives mirrored their paths through the heavens. (Frawley, 1994) The planets are the original *archetypes*.

In Vedic Astrology, the *navagraha,* or nine planets I am featuring in this book, represent a complete "spectrum" of human experience. They function similarly to the discernible colors of the color spectrum. Along the color spectrum, there are infinite hues between green and blue, but our eyes see green, and the next color they see is blue. Of course, we can also see aquamarine, teal, and so on, but we categorize them as versions of green or blue. Similarly, the planets are an elegant categorization of all human experience. I like to refer to the planets as "strands of energy" that exist within us and within all of life.

As specific strands of human experience, the planets show up in our lives in distinct ways.

We all have Mercury somewhere in our charts, showing us how our minds perceive our world and how we communicate. We tend to notice Mercury's "hue" in the *way* we communicate. Knowing Mercury's position in our charts can help reap some of the benefits and avoid the pitfalls that would otherwise take much trial and error to discover. It's like a cheat sheet for unlocking your highest potential.

For instance, say a person has Mercury in Aries in the seventh house. This might manifest in a tendency to draw really dynamic and sometimes combative people into their life. They might bemoan the fact that everybody is always trying to pick a fight with them, thinking, "Why can't we all just get along?" Understanding that Mercury in Aries in the seventh house has an evolutionary task of learning how to exist inside conflict for the sake of sustainable harmony helps that person stop projecting their expectation for others to show up a certain way. They can take responsibility for any passive aggressive communication tendencies and address any conflict avoidance that might exist. Mastering this part of their human experience might help them step into a role of mediator or speaker of difficult truths in an effort to bring deeper harmony to a situation.

As you will soon see, we will explore each of the nine planets' unique energy or category of human experience in depth. There are infinite numbers of celestial bodies *not* included in this book—the outer, generational, or "trans-Saturnian" planets Uranus, Neptune, and Pluto; the moons of other planets; asteroids, comets, and other dwarf planets; and so many more. While many of these celestial bodies are of enormous astrological significance, some of them even critical to the understanding of the birth chart, they are beyond the scope of this book.

A WORD ABOUT ASTROLOGICAL DIALECTS

Astrology is a language art, a storytelling form, a means of collective meaning making. As a language art, astrology has many different "dialects"—Hellenistic, Western, Vedic, Tajika, Chinese, Tibetan, Indigenous, and so on. Astrology can be spoken in many different ways.

Is any one language more "correct" than another? No, of course not. They have varying ways of communicating, that's all. When my clients ask me about whether the Vedic system I practice is "better" than Western Astrology, my response is, "I have studied both, and I happen to use the Vedic system primarily for working with people but use both systems in different applications."

And then I give them my Mac and PC analogy: Ultimately, both Mac and PC will generate a spreadsheet, get you online, write an email. But they go about it differently, and the user interface looks different as they perform the task at hand. In the end though, they both do the same job.

One of the fundamental differences between the Vedic and Western dialects is the amount of influence given to planets. The Vedic way of speaking about planets is as sovereign deities, beings with consciousness who influence our earthly lives. In this way, the Vedic perspective holds a highly animistic view of astrology. The Western way of relating with planets is that they don't have "influence" so much as they mirror our earthly lives.

The way the planets are described in this book transcends astrological "dialects" or systems. Most astrologers will agree with the spirit of what is presented about the planets, no matter which system they practice.

As a product of my personal experience, this book is a hybrid of different systems. My mother is from South India, and my father is from Germany. I am first-generation "American." My childhood took place in a multi-lingual context. Maybe this is why my brain tends to see things from the perspective of different languages simultaneously. I am often looking for the higher truth toward which both languages are attempting to point. I frequently function as a bridge between worlds.

By respecting each others' dialects and honoring the wisdom in the many approaches, we begin to crowdsource the solutions we desperately need at this point in our collective evolution.

AGENTS OF EVOLUTION

Our global problems will not be solved by someone else. Our global crises will be addressed by you and me, Agents of Evolution, acting independently, together.

If there's some part of you that knows your own enlightenment, or financial security, or family well-being, or even simple, personal enjoyment is not complete until everyone has achieved the same thing you have, then you have already intuited the ethos of this book.

By embarking on this book's voyage through our small solar system and making cultural meaning out of what it mirrors back to us, your awareness of your own unique part in our grand human symphony will become more clear to you. The result will be a step in our collective evolution.

Got your hats and sunscreen? Let's go!

PART I:

LUMINARIES

Sun and Moon
Day and Night
Father and Mother
Yang and Yin

Reveal for me
My inner light
My Soul's Truth
Illumine

We call the Sun and Moon "luminaries" because they are the two major heavenly sources of light on earth. Astrologically, they give rise to aspects of Consciousness that allow us to know ourselves.

Solar light reveals our identity in this world and represents how we shine outwardly in our lives.

Lunar light reveals our inner capacity to know what we feel; to know intimacy with others and with life; to know what makes us fulfilled, content, and happy.

Together, they illumine our awareness.

1

THE SUN: OUR
NEW NARRATIVE

———

"No sun outlasts its sunset, but it will rise again and bring the dawn."

—MAYA ANGELOU

CALL BACK THE SUN

One late summer morning, I sat at the electric keyboard in the cool of my cinder block basement, noodling with chords that felt good under my fingers. Something wanted to come through. I kept tinkering until one brave theme inside me lit up. I felt the whole song click into place as the other chords assembled themselves around that one central theme. It took courage to let that chord collection be themselves, not trying to make them sound like something I had heard before.

Sometimes it took lots of hours at the keyboard before some glimmer of recognition arose and I found what I was looking for. That day, though, the progression revealed itself quickly. I had taken Maya Angelou's poem "Caged Bird" and wrote music that seemingly fit. I had been obsessed with her poem for months, feeling it capture my emotional state at that time.

The song was alive in me. I dreamt about it. I heard it during random moments of the day. I moved toward it inside myself with tenderness, the way you might greet your own sweet child. This song-baby in turn made me feel so alive.

I enlisted the help of a gifted pianist and cellist. And this is when the magic really began to happen. During rehearsals, my body was in a perpetual state of goosebumps, listening to them breathe life into the skeleton of a song I put on their music stands. What an extraordinary sensation, to watch a faint idea become a living, breathing entity of its own.

Months later, the song was performed in an annual winter solstice dance performance, "Call Back the Sun." In the dark of the performance hall, supported by professional lights, sound, and costumes, the dancers danced an exquisite duo to "Caged Bird." The audience was rapt. With the song fully brought to life and received by its community, I felt the truth of me expressed.

Creation. Birth. Originality. Renewal. This is the Sun's cycle. By digging deep to be who we are, and expressing that at all costs, we shine the light of our true selves and brighten this world.

THE ASTROLOGICAL SUN

Light. Heat. Centrality. These are some of the qualities that astrologers have observed about the physical Sun. They give us understanding of what the Sun represents in our human lives. As Agents of Evolution, our relationship with what occupies the central place in our perspective is evolving. Where we assign sovereignty—who we allow to be the "the boss of me"—is evolving. Who is allowed to shine brightly is evolving. Who matters is evolving. These are all issues related to our collectively shifting hub, as represented by the astrological Sun.

The Sun speaks to our sovereignty.

Astrologers over the millennia have observed that the Sun represents these things about us: our authority, individuality, subjectivity, expressiveness, presence, vision, command, fatherhood, leadership, self-esteem, identity, royalty, self, selfishness, self-centeredness, and ability to "shine."

At one time in history, the sun represented the king, or the sovereign. As the American Federation of Astrologers explains, astrology was first used "as counsel for kings and emperors and, in time, for all of us." Our evolution as a human species has brought us to a point where we can grasp that most of us have sovereignty and some amount of agency within our individual lives. We generally understand that we shine our light and emit our warmth inside our own spheres of influence, whether that's in our home or workplace or communities or chosen families. We are each central in some circles, at least within ourselves. This sovereignty and agency we have is represented in the birth chart by the astrological Sun.

EVOLVING SOVEREIGNTY

As the societies we live in continually redefine who matters, our individual evolutionary paths around the Sun-oriented concepts of centrality, authority, and sovereignty also shift. For instance, for at least four hundred years here in the United States, centrality belonged unquestioningly to those humans of white skin color—an entirely arbitrary basis for centrality. That centrality has been challenged for a long time by the abolitionist movement and the civil rights movement and is slowly shifting, as can be evidenced today by the legislative success of the Black Lives Matter movement.

Centrality also standardly ran along lines of masculine gender, at least from the perspective of more recently written histories. This too is shifting, as more and more women work to birth their authentic selves into the world, claiming roles not standardly permitted for our gender, including election into public office.

Among those of us not living indigenous lifestyles, we humans have arbitrarily assumed centrality from among a vast, interconnected set of beings, including trees, animals, mountains, rivers, and the wind, to name a few. Out of necessity, this locus will also shift.

Shifts in identity are not easy for us as humans. Many alive today seemingly struggle to allow for a more nuanced, dimensional, and inclusive sense of identity to become central. Those struggling against this natural progression of identity and sovereignty hold onto old ideas of "self"— the Sun—outdated ideas that include dominance over, my centrality at the exclusion of yours, or me mattering at the expense of you.

Taking into account the good of the whole (all life on Earth), we now have a mandate to rediscover how centrality *actually* works. This will require that we give up our arbitrary, binary, flat assumptions of how centrality works. The Sun's path of evolution has to do with developing a new prototype for our capacity to transmit light, heat, and authority in our individual and collective lives, while considering and honoring our innate interdependence with *all* of life.

To begin, we can start by noticing the existing light and heat that is already there within ourselves. We learn what strengthens and weakens it. We might notice we are naturally drawn to spread our warmth and positive spirit and courage among our own family. From there, we might then observe that our own family either accepts and helps strengthen, or rejects or doesn't see or isn't able to receive our light, our warmth. We learn to "water where the grass grows," seeking out places that strengthen our Sun, choosing circles of beings in which our style of light is appreciated, where our warmth is welcomed, fully received, and reciprocated.

The nuclear family as the structure within which we must shine is no longer a necessity. Within our lifetimes, it is likely that a redistribution of *where* the light of our subjective self shines takes place (our role as sovereign) and that new structures sprout up to accommodate these new alliances (our kingdom). For example, "chosen family" may become more prominent than birth family. Or "intentional communities" may replace the original multi-generational living quarters that families once occupied.

How do we, as individuals, cocreate a world that works for everyone, all of us emitting heat and light, making space for all other bodies of light, balancing our own centrality within the complex systems in which we take part?

OPENING UP THE "WE" AS CENTRAL SPACE

American Integral philosopher Ken Wilber explores the evolution of what Integral Theory calls "We Space": "When we focus on a We Space, we are. . . by definition not focusing on the 'I.'"

Wilber talks about an inter-subjective field that unites all our subjective spaces and produces a kind of mirror space. This mirror space reflects each of our true selves *inside the We*. When we are able to drop into that kind of "group coherence," as he calls it, you and I would recognize we are part of a We. He goes on to explain that "each individual will still have a somewhat unique experience of the shared or collective We Space," because we'll each be looking at it from a different perspective.

A key to cocreating this world is that our sense of *collective identity* begins to shift to ever widening circles—rather than "we" or "us" referring to just my family, or the people of my same cultural heritage, or the people of my same socioeconomic bracket or level of education, or the people of my nation, or even to just humans, "we" and "us" refer more and more to all life on our planet. Until this happens, we are playing a zero-sum game where one person's win is another person's loss, or where taking something from one species or ecosystem is fine as long as it benefits me. Talk about a long-term losing proposition.

LEADERSHIP INSIDE THE "WE"

As a result of the collective shift in centrality, our current concept of leadership is naturally changing as well. In his closing remarks to the crowd assembled for a "Day of Mindfulness" event at Spirit Rock Center in October 1993, Thich Nhat Hanh famously proposed that the next Buddha may be a *sangha* (or spiritual community):

> *It is possible the next Buddha will not take the form of an individual. The next Buddha may take the form of a community, a community practicing understanding and lovingkindness, a community practicing mindful living. And the practice can be carried out as a group, as a city, as a nation.*

As we move toward this likelihood, it is my sense we will be learning what it looks like for communities to share authority and decision-making; to share leadership.

the revolving role of leadership among the 13 households of communal spirituality.

SUN'S DAWN

Between sundown and dawn, there is darkness. Who of us humans doesn't relate to the rhythm of this natural cycle? It is the same with all our identities. They brighten, they peak, then wane, then seemingly go out, only to brighten again in new ways. As we wake up to the global crises facing us, we will find we are at the dark point of a very long process *Trump's MAGA* of collective identity shift. We must look toward the dawn.

The path of evolution of the Sun has to do with how we define the center, how we define who we are, as a collective.

The Sun shines on everyone. How do we recognize ourselves as one people, one organism under the Sun? The evolutionary stage we are in collectively here in the West has less to do with becoming more individualized and more to do with creating pathways for interdependence.

Practice Pause

Spend a moment contemplating what this interdependence means for you, in practical terms.

Call to mind a big life decision you have to make soon. Take a few deep, long, slow breaths, focusing on your heart center. Make a prayer to the Sun that this decision resolves itself in the best way possible for the good of all beings. Stay here a moment and feel the Sun recognizing you for your unique quality of brilliance. Ask the Sun for their blessing for this decision. Stay with this until you feel an actual connection with the Sun in your heart. It may feel like a subtle shift in presence, or courage, or confidence. Thank the Sun, feeling the happiness that will come when your choice has been made, whenever that will be. Over the next days, weeks, months, see what happens as you make your decision and move forward with it.

CHANGING THE NARRATIVE

"An artist and an activist are not so far apart."

—AVA DUVERNAY, AWARD-WINNING WRITER,

PRODUCER, AND FILM DIRECTOR

Sun personalities are unmistakable. They are larger than life. They often dazzle. They exude energy, confidence, and heroism. Some of them are celebrities, or CEOs, or formally elected leaders. But most of them walk among us in our daily lives, inspiring people, empowering us, giving us courage to be our best selves, mobilizing us into action.

Ava DuVernay is the director of the film *Selma*, the documentary *13th*, the award-winning dramatic television series *Queen Sugar*, and the Netflix series *When They See Us*. Oprah says of DuVernay, "I've never seen anyone with such intense, passionate, willful, and clear direction, and yet be such a calming force as well." (Cipriani, 2014)

We look to leaders of our own choosing to help us formulate the narrative we want to work with. Control the narrative, and you can easily influence large groups. During a time when so many of our culturally held narratives haven't been updated in several hundred years, it feels remarkable when a new leader comes along with a new vantage point.

In a July 2020 interview given to the *New York Times*, DuVernay was asked about the role of storytelling in the political, cultural moment in which we found ourselves, just after George Floyd's murder. This is how she responded:

The story has been told from one point of view for too long. And when we say story, I don't just mean film or television. I mean the stories we embrace as part of the criminalization of Black people. Every time an officer writes a police report about an incident, they're telling a story. Look at the case of Breonna Taylor and her police report. They had nothing on it; it said she had no injuries. That is a story of those officers saying, 'Nothing to look at here, nothing happened.' But that's not the story that happened because if she could speak for herself, she would say, 'I was shot in the dark on a no-knock warrant in my bed.'

So, when you think of her story and multiply that times hundreds of thousands of people over the years in communities of color, specifically Black communities, a single story line has led the day, and we need to change that story line. And to do that, you have to change who the storytellers are.

As a heavily awarded, highly regarded, and prolific filmmaker, Ava DuVernay is not only changing who the storytellers are, she is changing the narrative. In the process, she changes how we see ourselves, how we know who we are. This is how Sun style leadership functions.

SHARING POWER

"Leadership is about empathy. It is about having the ability to relate to and connect with people for the purpose of inspiring and empowering their lives."

—OPRAH WINFREY

Catherine Parrish says when she started out as a school-teacher, what she really learned how to do was to listen. This was her strength. Today, Catherine is a leader's leader. She has served in leadership roles of several humanitarian organizations, including as CEO of the Hunger Project and as Chair of the Board at Pachamama Alliance, an organization whose mission is "to empower indigenous people of the Amazon rainforest to preserve their lands and culture and. . . to educate and inspire individuals everywhere to bring forth a thriving, just, and sustainable world."

I've known Catherine for over thirty years. My favorite memory of Catherine is seeing her once give a talk to a crowd when a butterfly landed on her shoulder. A visible gasp came over the whole audience. She just smiled and kept speaking as the butterfly stayed with her. The beauty of that moment was perfection—a kind of perfection and poise I associate with undeniable leadership. Undeniable because when animals, babies, or the natural world responds to someone with affection, you know you're in the presence of something special.

In addition to her leadership work within organizations, Catherine has also been a sought-after consultant to leaders and their organizations for the past twenty years. Working across the globe enabled her to witness emerging patterns in the way we collectively hold leadership.

Given the magnitude of what our world now confronts, I was specifically interested in hearing her talk on sharing leadership and sharing power. When I asked her what exactly was involved in this evolution toward shared leadership, she responded, "One could say that the Pachamama Alliance is working to discover or uncover the tenets of shared leadership, and to marry indigenous wisdom with the competence and intelligence of the systems designed in the so-called 'modern world' for the benefit, really, of a world that works for everyone."

LEADERSHIP IN PARTNERSHIP

Catherine shared with me that the practice of shared leadership and leading with listening was baked into the Pachamama Alliance's design since its inception in Ecuador by founders Bill and Lynne Twist. It was apparent to them that only if the indigenous residents and custodians of the rainforest who have safeguarded it were empowered would the greater human family be able to protect this pristine and vital "heart and lungs of the earth," upon which all human life and health depends. She says, "[Pachamama Alliance was] asked by the indigenous peoples to change the dream of the modern world. And we're working to do that through programs that awaken, educate, and inspire into action."

The Pachamama Alliance founders saw that the stewardship of the indigenous residents of the rainforest was succeeding, which was due in part to "their wisdom, their way of life, their way of thinking," as Catherine puts it. So, it became clear that the success of the mission to protect the rainforest wasn't going to happen by "teaching" the indigenous people, or bossing them around, or insisting they take up the model of what we in the Western world are doing to carry the day. Instead, it would be about listening and partnership.

The founders were invited to the Amazon by indigenous leaders, and so they went. The indigenous people they met told them from the beginning, "If you're here to help us, go home. If you're here because you see your future intertwined with ours, the well-being of your people, and the planet intertwined with ours, then you're welcome."

It was in that spirit of partnership that the Pachamama Alliance was born.

Catherine continues:

> *In partnership, there was that which we from the modern world could bring them that would empower their governance of the sacred headwaters of the Amazon rainforest, such as ability to communicate with their partner communities throughout this vast rain forest. And also, an ability to patrol their vast rain forest from intrusion of oil companies and other loggers and other illegal invaders. So, giving them drones and teaching them how to use [them], giving them financial support too, so that the leaders of the different communities could come together regularly and stay aligned and create a future vision for how to keep this rainforest pristine.*

> *If we are going to have Mother Earth regain her strength and power, we will need to work in this partnership.*

The Pachamama Alliance has an enduring commitment to stay true to this partnership. Part of their organization's official mission is to create an "environmentally sustainable, spiritually fulfilling, and socially just" world for all.

"That's a tall order," I tell Catherine. "How do we do that?"

"It's a constant inquiry," she counsels. "And the discipline is to stay in the inquiry."

EVOLUTIONARY COMPETENCIES: SUN BEAMS

The Sun represents the primordial creative force within us. As we create, our identity changes. As our identity changes, the game we're playing changes. As the game we're playing changes, life on Earth changes.

We do not need to be in formal positions of leadership to lead. Since there are many levels of conscious beingness inhabiting the earth simultaneously, with no guarantee that official leadership roles will be inhabited by the most evolved among us, those interested in being part of our collective evolution must *out-create* the ones sowing destruction.

DISCOVERING WHO WE REALLY ARE

In *Conscious Business*, Fred Kofman encourages business leaders to find out: "Who is it that I really am?" He makes a case for not just superficially looking into things like strengths and weaknesses or what we love, but to go deeper. Way deeper. Deep enough to get to the source of what we truly are, what lies there behind our eyes and vision, quietly witnessing everything:

> *See, if I'm going to be in the world without the fear and the danger of being insulted, I need to find out what is it that I am. What is it that cannot be insulted? What is it that can achieve unconditional success, even in the face of apparent failure? That kind of entity is what lies at the source of my humanity... What I want to do is go as far as*

we can into the roots of this phenomenon of consciousness and find out: What is its seed? Where does the conscious human being come from? And what is its ultimate essence?

. . . This quest is not just a spiritual quest. It is also a very practical business question. The more identified we are with things that are not true, the less able we will be to communicate, to coordinate our actions, and to learn.. . . Finding out who I really am and aligning my beliefs about myself with the true nature of myself is going to become a very, very fundamental business imperative.

A NEW HERO, A NEW MYTH

Culturally, we cocreate our heroes. Our collective consciousness spins together new forms of heroes to match the new problems we continually face. In a conversation with Bill Moyers in *The Power of Myth*, Joseph Campbell speaks about myth in this way:

Mythology is not a lie, mythology is poetry, it is metaphorical. It has been well said that mythology is the penultimate truth—penultimate because the ultimate cannot be put into words. It is beyond words. Beyond images, beyond that bounding rim of the Buddhist Wheel of Becoming. Mythology pitches the mind beyond that rim, to what can be known but not told.

On the frontiers of our collective evolution are the mythmakers. Those artists and mothers, mystics and meditators, cultural philosophers and farmers can see beyond what the world presents and pull out the emerging stories and heroes. Once we can clearly see the problems, we can blueprint the new heroes and heroines required. The solutions emerge through the heroines *we dream up.*

Writing Prompt

Try your own hand at authoring a new narrative in this fun, simple way. First, call to mind a particular world crisis. If the world crisis were a villain, what kind of villain would it be? Picture this villain in your mind's eye.

Now set your timer for five minutes and write the narrative for a comic book, creating a superhero who comes in to battle that villain. What superpowers do they have? Who are their allies? What early wounds have they healed to reveal their great strength, uniquely positioning them to vanquish the villain?

MYTH AS MEDICINE

As fire, heat, warmth, and light, the Sun creates life. The Sun is also associated with great stories, no matter what form they take—a novel, a play, a movie, a dream. Stories are creative in the literal sense—they blueprint our world.

Stories about who we are, stories about what life is, stories about other people—these stories will define how we see ourselves connected to everything in our lives. If it is not in our story, we will tend to be unconscious in relationship with it. Which is why, right now, we need myths that see us as part of the one organism that is Planet Earth rather than the old myth of "us" versus "them."

Joseph Cambell says:

> *Myth basically serves four functions. The first is the mystical function. . . realizing what a wonder the universe is, and what a wonder you are, and experiencing awe before this mystery.. . . The second is a cosmological dimension, the dimension with which science is concerned—showing you what shape the universe is, but showing it in such a way that the mystery again comes through.. . . The third function is the sociological one—supporting and validating a certain social order.. . . It is the sociological function of myth that has taken over in our world—and it is out of date.. . . But there is a fourth function of myth, and this is the one that I think everyone must try today to relate to—and that is the pedagogical function, of how to live a human lifetime under any circumstances.*

During our lifetimes, we may find we need stories to keep us going. We may come upon impossible times. The stories we tell ourselves can and will help us frame why and how we keep going.

THE UNIVERSE IS THE CENTER OF THE UNIVERSE

Shortly after performing the music I had written to accompany the dancers, my own life imploded. This is often how it goes with writing a new story. The old story has to die first. The dance company founder left our small town and moved to Mexico. I grieved that loss terribly. She had been a dear friend, one of the few in my town I could relate to as an artist. My marriage was dissolving. My financial life was in ruins. I had entered my "dark night of the Soul." But some new identity was fighting to be uncaged. Authoring my own new narrative required vision, boldness, and courage. I didn't always feel up to it. Eventually, that new narrative dawned.

As the hero of your story, what kind of heroism is your life calling forth? You may not have many role models for this type of heroism. Why? Because it might not exist yet. You are authoring it.

Our universe has an infinite number of centers, depending on who is telling the story. As we each author the individually emerging new story, we automatically move the needle on our collective evolution.

2

MOON: CRADLE
OF BELONGING

———

"When the heart is right, the mind and the body will follow."

"Women, if the Soul of the nation is to be saved, I believe that you must become its Soul."
—CORETTA SCOTT KING

CARE PACKAGE

Staring at the shadows dancing on my bed, I sat in my college dorm room, bereft. I searched hard in that moment to find comfort. I was excited to be in my first semester away at school and was making friends easily enough, but it was hard to relax, hard to concentrate. Everything was new, with sharp edges and a steep learning curve. The November light coming through my dorm window formed monochromatic shadows on my sleeping bag, giving me something to focus on as my mind drifted.

"I'm not sure I belong here. I stand out like a sore thumb. I don't dress like these people, my skin is darker than theirs, and I don't like their food." I was having to learn a whole new code of interaction. I rubbed my fingers along the rough white nylon seams of the blue and red synthetic sleeping bag my dad got me from an army surplus supply.

Heading to answer a knock at the door, I heard, "Package for you," as the door opened and one of my dorm-mates walked in smiling. I took the package from her hands and saw my mother's familiar handwriting and held back big tears. But as soon as I closed the door and brought the package to my bed, one of three beds in the small room, my stomach began trembling. It poured out now, long sobs of sadness over all that was not here in this moment with me: my sisters and brother, my mother and father, our dogs, the home that I loved, the street where so much of my childhood had happened, the way the light came in the beveled glass flanking our front door creating rainbows on the wine-red carpet. It would never again return. My childhood was gone. I was growing up, and the finality of it was tearing me in two.

As I opened the package, delicately placing its contents on my sleeping bag, I felt a waft of protection and warmth, like the smell from the kitchen the day my mother made blueberry muffins for me before a speech tournament. A box of my favorite windmill cookies, sweeter because she knew they were my favorite; a bar of soap whose familiar scent brought rivulets of pleasure; a tiny Christmas angel that would remind me of the good times we had all shared; and some flannel pajamas, soft and comforting. All these wrapped up with my mother's care. I saw her hands touching these same objects, placing them in the box to send, and felt her touch consoling me now.

I would never be able to climb back into my childhood. While nothing would be exactly the same when I returned to 1611 Coursin Street, my mother's care package brought me home for a few moments on that cold, November day. Reconnecting me with all that I held dear, returning me to my sense of the familiar, she reminded me that there was a place I would always belong and that everything was going to be okay.

Moon experiences are like this. The Moon is the home within us, our inner true north, a deep and intimate sense of who we are, arising out of a feeling of being loved and wanted, a knowing that we belong.

THE ASTROLOGICAL MOON

The Moon has fascinated, soothed, terrified, enchanted, and bewitched humans since time immemorial. In the language of astrology, the Moon points to our inner knowing about life and relationship. It is our feeling nature, the dimension of perception that tells us if we feel safe, secure, welcomed. It lets us know when intimacy is present and points to our emotional intelligence and our capacity to connect.

The Moon shows us our capacity for intimacy with life.

The Moon in a chart shows how easily we trust others and whether that trust is well placed. The Moon is feminine, dark, *Yin*, receptive. The Moon's placement in a chart shows each individual's patterns, trends, and ancestral inheritances around intimacy. It comments on our first intimacy in life— with our mother.

EVOLVING INTIMACY

The Moon is perhaps the most exciting part of the chart to work with. Since the Moon travels faster through the zodiac than any of the other astrological planets, our experience of the Moon is always changing anyway and, therefore, relatively easy to evolve. The Moon responds quickly and easily to our intention to change. With the Moon, we can feel encouraged, empowered even, by fast results. If I want to change how I feel, I can think a different thought, and I will feel different. It's a subtle, fake-it-til-you-make-it manipulation that works with our pliable moonscapes.

Walking the Moon's path might *seem* easy because of quick successes. Don't be fooled. Moon work is the most dimensional of all the paths. Here we meet all our emotional resistances to true transformation. Much individual talk therapy is structured to address the path of the Moon. Walking this path requires first becoming aware of what we feel, and even this first step can be tricky.

The Moon is also astrologically associated with our memory. Under the Moon, how we remember, and possibly what we choose to remember, is related to our capacity for intimacy. Negative memory erodes intimacy through the mistrust that can often accompany it. Negative memory can thwart personal evolution because of how it isolates us and keeps us separate—the opposite movement to lunar evolution. Therefore, it is important to be able to examine all our implicit biases, all the conscious and maybe even subconscious programs running inside us, telling us who is safe, who is a friend, who belongs.

The evolutionary path of the Moon is all about developing greater intimacy with all of life.

One of the primary developments needed for this intimacy involves coming to see life, reality, events, and relationships *as they are*, with no perceptual aliases attached. This is a tall order for a human being. Most of our sense of security and safety comes from social codes established from infancy, about who is a friend, who is a threat, how to behave in different situations. For some of us, fight, flight, and freeze trauma responses may also be stored in our somatic memory, another province of the Moon. And some of the implicit biases these social codes and trauma responses engender can utterly block our ability to see things as they are.

The practice of seeing things as they are doesn't mean we ignore the social codes we've been taught. Although some of them are destructive, many of them are useful. Seeing things as they are just lets us acknowledge the overlay of social codes on the intimacy of a moment so we don't lose touch with that intimacy.

Our lunar experience is primordial. Our mammalian brain is wired for connection. Evolving our Moon capacity is less about reaching for something beyond us and more about relaxing and accepting, welcoming what's already brilliantly at work within us, much like a loving mother accepts and welcomes her children.

CREATOR'S MOON: THE BABY WHISPERER

The Moon represents motherhood in all its dimensions. Just as there are many kinds of mothers in the world, there are many different expressions of the astrological Moon. Some expressions of the Moon are soft and nurturing. Other expressions are oriented toward cultural preservation. Still other Moons express as fierce protectors, like mother bears. The single thread woven through these differing expressions of the Moon is mothering.

What follows next are three stories of three distinctly different expressions of the Moon.

Kama Tai Mitchell's story is a story as old as creation itself, weaving on down to her through her lineage grandmothers. Kama's family calls her on the phone when their own babies are crying. She has the ability to take one listen to the baby, gather a sense of what's going on, and tell the adults what they might try in order to soothe the baby. She's been doing this since she herself was a kid, because even then she had the ability to communicate, non-verbally, with babies. Her family calls her the baby whisperer.

I got to know Kama when she facilitated an online group in which I participated. I experienced the way she held a space of unconditional acceptance. Her vibe always communicated to me, "You are loved. You are welcomed here. Isn't this fun that we get to do this together?" Though our online group had never met in person, it felt like a large family.

Kama is a mother of two. About a year after she had her second child, Kama was invited to be present at a home birth.

She knew nothing about being a doula, but friends and other doulas and midwives could tell she had a sixth sense for it. She describes that birth as "serene" and "divine." The woman giving birth "did the whole no-pushing, natural reflux of baby." This experience lit a flame in Kama for doing birth work. Fifty births later, she got her doula certification.

In Michigan, doulas are paid out of pocket for home births since they're not covered by insurance. And because of that Kama remembers, "A lot of my first births were with wealthier white women." In Kalamazoo at that time, Kama reports that Black babies were dying at a rate four times greater than white babies, yet Black people were only thirteen percent of the population. Knowing that doula care would support Black and Brown mothers in feeling safe, supported, and nurtured through the experience of childbirth and early motherhood, and therefore would likely have a beneficial effect on the infant mortality rate, Kama longed for Black and Brown women to have access to doula care.

Kama remembers waking to the need for a solution when a new CEO from Uganda joined the local Young Women's Christian Association (YWCA) leadership. This fierce new woman CEO was shocked at the disparity between the white versus Black and Brown infant mortality rates in the Kalamazoo community and called a conference to look at the issues. Kama remembers, "She basically said, 'This is a direct correlation to the health of our overall community. We have to fix this.'"

Though Kama was brand new to the birth work scene at that time, she immediately saw how hospitals tended to place the blame for the infant mortality rates on Black people. She explained that while doctors and nurses don't say it outright, "there's always a spin: 'Well, you know, I'm a home visiting nurse, and they don't want me to come in their house,' or 'They keep canceling their appointments,' or 'They don't get prenatal care.' What they're really saying is, 'Black people don't know what they're doing. They don't know how to show up. They don't take the resources that we're offering them.'"

Kama understood something about the situation intuitively. She knew it wasn't about Black people rejecting resources: "This is a socioeconomic issue. Point blank. We have a medical system with two hundred hospitals in this community, all these resources, but there's a racial trust issue. There's not one Black OB-GYN or midwife in all of Southwest Michigan, and until I came about, there were no black doulas."

In 2015, after participating in many well-intentioned meetings led by an inter-organizational effort called Cradle Kalamazoo—whose mission was to end infant mortality—Kama grew weary of advocating for the need for doulas to serve the Black and Brown communities. She offered presentations and attended meetings, but ultimately she realized, "They're not hearing me. I'm wasting my time. I'm just gonna go do the work."

So, Kama gathered other Black women and funded their doula training with a grant. "We just went and did the work," she says.

Kama's organization, Rootead, provided the birth work her own community needed. Their mission statement encapsulates the classic drives the Moon inspires: "Reclaiming the village through cultural liberation by holding spaces for internal transformation, healing arts, and birthing justice."

Rootead's impact on births in the Black community soon captured the interest of others in Michigan, including Cradle Kalamazoo. "Then it was like, 'Come sit at our table and tell us your methodology,'" Kama remembers.

Rootead's story is a Moon Love story. Love and nurturing and connection and belonging are a legacy given to us by our mothers. This legacy gets passed down from generation to generation. Yet, because its impact most frequently happens under the radar, in back rooms and in the more subtle realms of home and hearth, the Moon's presence often takes a back seat to the Sun in our current Western culture, not receiving much fanfare or recognition.

Today Rootead is thriving, offering birth work services and a rich array of cultural experiences, such as African dance for youth. I bet Kama's grandmothers are proud.

SUSTAINER'S MOON: "DON'T BROWN BAG IT!"

The Moon is about the continuity of culture, and though she rules the Past, she is also about renewal. In the same way that a woman's womb renews itself with cleansing blood every month during her "Moon," the lunar forces among us cyclically revitalize our capacity to connect with each other and with the Earth.

Agnes Baker Pilgrim was a beloved and formidable Takelma Tribe native elder. To all in the southern Oregon area where she lived, she was affectionately known as "Grandma Aggie."

I watched her perform a water blessing at a hotel and spa resort built atop natural mineral springs. She swished her fingers through the bowl of water, speaking prayers over it, pouring water from other smaller vessels into the larger bowl. Soon, the small band of us assembled would go outside to a natural mineral spring where Grandma Aggie would bless all the unified waters in a spirit of gratitude.

It was December 2016. I was working for the hotelier on whose land these natural springs currently bubbled up. Long before ownership of land was a thing, Native Americans came to these waters for healing. Feeling guilty to be witnessing this act of graciousness when so much had been stolen from her people by newcomers like me, I asked her, "Grandma Aggie, how is it that you don't hold a grudge about this situation? How are you able to come here and bless the waters?"

"Oh, now don't go carryin' that old nonsense with you everywhere. Don't brown bag it!" she replied.

"What do you mean, don't brown bag it?" I asked, perplexed.

"Don't take that old history around with you like a paper bag lunch!"

Because I'd previously witnessed how Grandma Aggie's fierce voice for maintaining the cultural integrity of native traditions impacted large gatherings, her answer went straight through to my heart. Rather than focusing on the land that had been taken, she was teaching me to renew and revitalize on an even deeper level, a property of water itself. The hoteliers considered themselves stewards of those mineral springs, and as Grandma Aggie was their friend, her heart was clear. She didn't allow the past to fester in her inner emotional space.

Before her death in late 2019, Grandma Aggie was one of thirteen native grandmothers on the International Council of Thirteen Grandmothers, a global alliance of indigenous elders coming together for prayer, education, and healing, nurturing their cultures through preservation and protection of lands, medicines, language, and ceremonial ways of prayer. She was also a water protector, a job she devotedly performed through her eighties and nineties. Her message was simple and crystal clear:

Spirit said, all humans came from water in the amniotic sac of our mother's womb, and that Water is our first medicine. We are to take care of it and guard it. Not just for now but for seven generations to come in the unborn.

The astrological Moon cares about how clean and clear we keep our emotional space, or the astrological element of water. The physical manifestation of our collective emotional space is the water on our planet. Grandma Aggie explains that gratitude and blessing must be our first approach to water:

I found out water can hear. So, talk to the water inside of you, and thank it for your life.

When I'm standing in the shower, "Bless me. I love you."

When I'm driving my car over a bridge of water anywhere in the world, I say, "Bless you water. Thank you for all that lives in you and drinks from your banks." And I thank it in that way.

Us humans, us two-leggeds are the caretakers of this planet. It is our job.

Water collectively flows in one direction. We can take a cue from water and flow united in our protection of it. Grandma Aggie's teaching legacy lives on. She will always remain a grandmother to all whose lives she touched.

Practice Pause:

Try Grandma Aggie's suggestion. For the next week, when you interact with water, thank and bless it. Lifting a glass of water, say, "Thank you, I love you." When you cross a bridge in your car, tell the water, "Thank you, I love you." Watch what this does to your awareness of the preciousness of water.

PROTECTOR'S MOON: MATRIARCHAL CULTURE

"There are those of us who are content to assimilate or whatever, but there are those of us who want to maintain the culture our ancestors died for.... We have the right to be who we are."

—MADONNA THUNDER HAWK, 2008

The Moon is soft, but she can also be fierce, like a mother bear. The maternal urge to protect is part of the lunar experience.

Intergenerational trauma runs rife through the experience of Native American mothers from five hundred plus years of the United States government abandoning treaties, forced sterilizations, and mass relocations to Native American boarding schools where children wrested from their mothers were violently assimilated into colonial culture. Such fires intensify the Native mother's protective instincts.

Madonna Thunder Hawk is a member of the Oohenumpa band of the Cheyenne River Sioux Tribe, and she grew up on the Cheyenne River Sioux Reservation. She experienced first-hand the systemic violence and government intrusion into Native life that was common treatment during her generation. She is known as a formidable force in Native activism.

"You know our ancestors lived in a matriarchal society, and so when colonization came that changed all that," she says. But still, the matriarchy is alive and well today for her Lakota people during everyday life, where the influence of the grandmother weaves the values and language and culture through the generations. Matriarchy also activates at critical moments, "when things happen, like under stress and duress and a camp forms, it's automatic that the matriarchal system kicks in. It's for survival. And that's who we are—we're survivors," says Thunder Hawk.

Alongside her daughter, Marcella Gilbert, Madonna Thunder Hawk was present at the protest against the Dakota Access Pipeline at Standing Rock (a.k.a. DAPL). (Castle, 2018) A direct affront to the Lakota Sioux ways, the pipeline threatens the water of the region and desecrates their sacred sites. The protest, begun by youth, quickly became an encampment where thousands from around the country gathered in solidarity with the Standing Rock tribe. The aggressive military action taken against the protestors was extreme and shameful, leaving many to be re-traumatized by the ongoing effects of colonization.

Standing Rock was only one event in a lifetime of Native activism for Thunder Hawk, exemplifying the powers of matriarchy. Among other notable achievements, she founded the "We Will Remember" Survival School in the 1970s as a Native alternative to government-run education. As the documentary film *Warrior Women* portrays, Madonna Thunder Hawk's activism continues to be passed down in a powerful matriarchal lineage through her daughter Marcella, now a mother herself.

Matriarchal culture is quintessentially lunar. The strength of the Moon is in the cultural connection woven from generation to generation, through the women. Some cultures can do this weaving in soft, protected spaces, but when a culture's women are forced to protect their ways in hostile environments, they necessarily become warriors.

Under a colonial mindset, however, a woman doesn't have sovereignty over her own body, or over the way she chooses to care for or educate her child. In an *Our Bodies, Ourselves* blogpost, Amie Newman writes, "Native American cultures traditionally support and respect women's autonomy with regard to reproductive health decisions. It is only since Native cultures were colonized by white people that traditional healing practices, particularly those led by women for women, become marginalized."

During the Dakota Access Pipeline protest at Standing Rock, in true Moon fashion, life continued. Babies were born. One of the indigenous midwives present during that historic protest offers us this insight about the connection between caring for Mother Earth and supporting women and women's health: "We've come with a group of women to be able to support women's health here at the encampment. Sovereignty for indigenous people is only going to come about through the support of women and women's health, in the same way that we defend and protect Mother Earth is the same way that we need to defend and protect women and the next generations of children being born." (Newman, 2016)

Not everyone has what it takes to stand unarmed in front of heavily equipped military personnel in order to defend all that we hold sacred. But every single one of us can respect and lift up those grandmothers among us who do.

EVOLUTIONARY COMPETENCIES: TENDRILS OF THE MOON

Intimacy and belonging are the domain of the Moon. In losing our connection to our original mother, the Earth, many of us in the global North are losing our capacity for intimacy and our sense of connection with each other. The following suggestions offer practices and attitudes by which you can cultivate these critical Moon skills.

EVOLVING EMPATHY

Empathy without boundaries is an ocean without shores. Flooding will happen. It is critical for those beings among us with a heightened capacity for empathy (being an "empath" is a lunar talent) to strengthen our ability to turn on and turn off the valve regulating our empathic flow. Empathy in a toxic world leads to poisoning of the whole system. It's much better to understand where your limits are and when it is time to pull back, cleanse, and recharge.

Our culture does not favor lunar types, whether man or woman. Western culture does not understand or value the lunar "work" empathic humans perform on behalf of all. Like Grandma Aggie charging the waters with gratitude and reciprocity on behalf of all, tending to empathically derived material in our own emotional waters is critical. Cleansing and healing happen in private, during quiet time, in relaxation, and in the natural world. We have to give these spaces to ourselves, regardless of whether the world around us supports that imperative. You wouldn't *not* bathe your body. Similarly, when you have taken on a load of empathic material from another person or from the collective, it is important to bathe, cleanse, and revitalize the personal energy body.

DIVERSIFY OUR COMMUNITIES

More and more, we come into contact with people not of our own race, or socioeconomic status, or educational background, or political persuasion. I asked Kama what she would suggest as a practice to promote intimacy and belonging among the entire human family. Her response was simple: "Show up even when it's hard and uncomfortable."

We can grow our own inner comfort with those different from ourselves. We can bring ourselves more and more to places that are uncomfortable while being gentle with ourselves, like a mother tending to a distraught child. What do we do when the discomfort shows up? We don't push it away. We can form an inner commitment to be open to others who are beyond our comfort zone. Kama suggests: "Be straight up. Be authentic. Be willing to be vulnerable—admit your discomfort."

BE A WATER PROTECTOR
The Lakota phrase *Mni Wiconi* means "water is life." The water on our precious Mother Earth belongs to all of us. We must protect the waters of the Mother as if our lives depended on it, because they do: up to 60 percent of the adult human body consists of water. (USGS) What will it take for us to become aware of how sacred water is?

Begin by becoming aware of all of your interactions with water on a daily basis. Count how many times in a day you come into contact with water, whether for drinking, for bathing, for cooking, for cleaning, for plants, for pets, when it's raining, or when you see a body of water. Bless the water each time you interact with it. What is the commitment that naturally arises for you around protecting our precious water?

Writing Prompt

All Moon work begins with being intimately familiar with your inner emotional landscape. The practice of writing or journaling often works to help you explore and discover that terrain. Try setting a timer for ten minutes and answer this question: "What does my feeling body want to tell me today?"

Put pen to paper and don't stop. Write gibberish if you get stuck. Just write whatever comes to your mind. Once the ten minutes are up, put away what you've written and revisit it a little later in the day. You might be able to connect some dots for yourself.

GETTING BACK TO THE ROOT

When I asked Kama Tai what she thought would get us back to a world where everyone belongs, she stressed the importance of getting back to our roots: "None of this new stuff that we love [like new forms of music and dance] would be here without the traditional stuff. We have to know our roots." In keeping with remembering traditions, Kama's organization, Rootead, offers African dance opportunities for the young people of her community. This is Moon wisdom. To move forward, we must root more deeply into where we came from. When we skip this step, we forget ourselves.

Coming together in diverse spaces has the potential to instill in us even more appreciation for what we bring to the group—the glorious legacies handed down to us by our ancestors and traditions; the wisdom; the resilience; the resource. When we are aware of our own roots, we have more to offer to diverse spaces.

HOW TO INCLUDE

The act of including others is straight up about love and care. Being willing to come together in all our diversity demonstrates our love and care for our human family. Coming together in diversity with love and care is the domain of the Moon.

The fact that my mother knew exactly which cookies to send me in her care package all those decades ago spoke of her love and care. She had to notice what I liked, what I responded to. This act of paying attention is something we can do for each other, even when (maybe especially when) the person we're doing it for comes from a completely different background.

Evolving the Moon is us collectively paying more attention to "them"—anyone we wouldn't initially put in our own circle of "us." Like with that most famous reindeer of all, paying attention means not just inviting Rudolph to our reindeer games, but finding out what kind of reindeer games *they* like to play, then creating community experiences where "they" become one of "us."

Who's outside your circle of people you feel comfortable with? How will you include them?

PART II:

PERSONAL PLANETS

Mercury, Venus, and Mars
Jewels among the stars
The way I am
I was born to be
You light up
My personality

Because their orbits around the Sun and around the zodiac are relatively quick (less than three earth months for Mercury, less than eight Earth months for Venus, and less than two Earth years for Mars), the personal planets represent the most readily visible part of the human organism—the individual. From the individual, the human organism moves out into the family, the culture and nation, and the generations.

The personal planets give rise to our individual personalities as distinct from the influences of family, culture and nation, and generations. Most of what we think of as "personality traits" are products of these planets.

3

MERCURY: OUR BEAUTIFUL MIND

"For things to reveal themselves to us, we need to be ready to abandon our views about them."

—THICH NHAT HANH

QUOTING COLTRANE

Transfixed by the sound of the trumpet, I sat in the dark concert hall overcome with emotion. What was at first a mild tightness in my chest slowly stretched itself out in sweet release. Thoughts collided as they vied for my attention—a random memory of fireflies on a late summer evening, heated words exchanged with a boyfriend, the sounds of gossip from the coffee shop across the street from the concert hall where I would meet a friend later to gab and people watch. The music took me there.

Each phrase coming from the trumpet pressed on some other tender place in my Soul, extruding all my unbearable pains and joys out through time. The friend whose senior recital it was sang to us wordlessly through his trumpet. This wail a sorrowful mourn, that jabber a joyful tête-à-tête, the next squawk an impatience. His shapes cascaded, tumbled, somersaulted, cartwheeled through the air. Without uttering a word, he carried on a conversation with other members of his ensemble for us to overhear, taking inventory on life as he pushed air through his horn. At times he "quoted" other great musicians—now Coltrane, now Miles—and at moments in the pieces he straight up "gave a speech." We, his assembled listeners, were rapt by what he was "saying." His music told us what it felt like to be him. It gave us encouragement and medicine for our own lives. But most of all, he touched us.

Not a word had been spoken but the audience was visibly moved. The whole experience left indelible impressions far beyond my junior year college self. Not so much because of what was "said," but because of the wondrousness of saying a thing.

This is the power of Mercury—to share the vast range of all possible human experience with others.

THE ASTROLOGICAL MERCURY

Equated with the fleet-footed Greek god Hermes, Mercury in the astrological birth chart represents what we commonly think of as the Mind. His placement in our chart describes a thing or two about how we communicate, how accurately we balance our checkbook, how quickly we remember people's names. When Mercury is strong, we're quick, we're funny, we're organized, we're rational, and probably also affable, if not downright likeable.

Mercury is related to the mind.

Mercury is curious, childlike, changeable, and easily influenced. Put Mercury with a Saturn-like authority, and Mercury becomes scientific, needing proof, being wed to reason. Put him with someone like Venus and you might get a well-dressed popular comedian or a talkative retailer making a killing over the most sought-after merchandise in town.

Often referred to as a trickster—his preferred role when in his *retrograde* period—Mercury loves all word plays and rearrangements and hiding and tricking that get our knickers in a twist. He can be a rascal that way. He loves a good game.

Mercury tag teams with Venus to create all trends in popular culture. Get the two of them together and you have a best-selling novel, the funniest meme ever, or next year's fashions.

Social conventions are also Mercury's domain (again, slightly in partnership with Venus). After hearing twenty times, "Don't be rude!" from our mother, we might refrain in the future from whatever behavior was considered to be rude. Mercury strives to learn the rules of any game, particularly the social game of conversation, for the pleasure of interacting.

Mercury does not show up in the same way for everyone. There is a different growth plan or evolution available to the cheetah, the monkey, the spider, and the hawk. Similarly, our human selves have vastly different perception styles, capacities, and interests. Our use of these Mercurial gifts is a function of the culture we were born into, the language (or languages) we were taught to think inside, and the life circumstances accompanying us at birth.

DEEPER DIMENSIONS OF MERCURY

Below the surface, Mercury influences how we perceive our world. Mercury functions as a bridge between us and the rest of life. In classical Vedic Medical Astrology, the planet Mercury is linked to our nervous system as well as our skin— both of which help our brains sort out the world around us and ourself in relation to it. This often-hidden set of perceptions is all part of Mercury's wheelhouse.

The ability to sense and perceive our environment in a full-bodied way unfolds during every waking moment, even though we only see the summation of these complex processes in what a person chooses to present to us. For instance, when we meet a stranger, our entire body senses the other person's body and presence in the environment and goes through endless complex computations about whether this person is friend or foe, whether this person is valuable, and so on. No readout of the complex processes in our individual brains is made available to anyone, but we broadcast the summation of those decisions anyway through our interactions—by our body language, by how confident and relaxed we appear, by how easily we smile, and, of course, by what we say.

Mercury's primary gift to us is the power of blueprinting. Through Mercury, we craft what we want to experience; we can craft a world just by defining its specs. Mercury offers us mastery of this power through regular, steady effort. I remember reading a book called *Creative Visualization*, by Shakti Gawain, when I was living in New York. I practiced the (Mercury) techniques in that book to manifest going on a national tour as a musician. Because our thoughts blueprint our realities, putting regular effort into visualizing something you want can help make it happen.

Also in the Mercury camp is a skill we now commonly refer to as "mindfulness." Here in the West, we often credit Thich Nhat Hanh, Jon Kabat-Zinn, and others with popularizing the practice of *mindfulness*. Essentially, mindfulness is being present to *what is*.

Our individual Mercury function benefits enormously from cultivating mindfulness. It's one of the super simple things we can do on the daily to help along Mercury's evolution in our own lives.

Practice Pause:

The breath is a potent aid for assisting us in bringing all of ourselves into the present moment. Try this simple yet profound mindfulness exercise often referred to as "Box Breathing" to get a taste of what it feels like to recruit all of yourself to be here:

Close your eyes if it helps you to be present.

Breathe in to a count of four through your nose.

Suspend the breath for a count of four, keeping your mouth closed.

Breathe out for a count of four through your nose.

Suspend the breath for a count of four.

Repeat this a few times and see if you notice a change in how present you are.

EVOLVING PERCEPTION

"The hardest thing of all to see is what is really there."

—J. A. BAKER

Have you ever made up your mind about a situation based on all the data available to you, and then later found out the truth of the situation was altogether different from what you thought it was? Such is the nature of truth. It depends on what information and awareness we have available to us.

Mercury is tricky this way. As the planet of speech, communication, and the mind, Mercury arrives at relative truths every waking minute. But is there such a thing as an absolute truth?

The worldviews we inhabit are paradigms that, as Agents of Evolution, we would be smart to examine. Closer inspection often reveals them to be a flimsy, ragtag assortment of unchallenged familial and cultural beliefs we swallowed whole. These worldviews get us into heaps of trouble, especially the unexamined ones.

Not only are our unexamined worldviews limiting, often we find out they're straight up wrong. What might we be dead wrong about *right now*? Every society before us has experienced this. Sometime between the fifteenth and seventeenth centuries the idea of a flat Earth finally fell out of favor, even though Pythagoras and others had spoken about a spherically shaped Earth since the sixth century BC. That one factually incorrect belief radically limited our imaginations about ourselves and what was possible. Chances are that right now, we actively believe something just as limiting.

What if at this point in human history, the greatest unknown frontiers are not in the physical world, but within—truths about ourselves and about the human species, about our human perception, and communication? What if discovering these truths radically shifts our imagination about what is possible, just like spherical Earth must have for early sixteenth century Europe? What new understandings are already alive, living, and breathing among us that will change our concept of ourselves forever?

I predict that our greatest future discoveries lie in *the way we think and process information.*

A POST-LITERATE WORLD

"We live, we die, and like the grass and trees, renew ourselves from the soft Earth of the grave. Stones crumble and decay, faiths grow old and they are forgotten, but new beliefs are born. The faith of the villages is dust now.... but it will grow again... like the trees."

—CHIEF JOSEPH, NEZ PERCE

Regardless of the particular way we dance the Mercury dance in our lives, our human collective is progressing in a decidedly non-literary way. I remember the day I heard author Seth Godin talk to a group of writers about a "post-literate world." It was shocking. At first I thought, *Whoa, did I hear him right? A post-literate world?* I googled it. Sure enough, there it was, ironically *in print* on his blog: "As we race toward a post-literate world. . . " My palms sweat, and my stomach got queasy. I considered what I just heard. A post-literate society would mean we no longer center literature or the written word. Reading and writing would be obsolete.

Yes, I had to admit to myself, *this is already happening.* The information age has us all needing the soundbite, reaching for the instant download to our brains, getting our news as much from social media as from journalism outlets, watching a video over reading a how-to. Seth is right. A post-literate world does indeed seem on the horizon (or perhaps, it's already arrived). So, what does Mercury become in a post-literate society?

No stranger to shapeshifting, Mercury will still represent all our avenues for communication, whatever they shapeshift into, long after books go the way of the dinosaur.

FROM WAITRESS TO CONGRESS
We stand to learn a thing or two about the collective evolution of our Mercury function from Alexandria Ocasio-Cortez's (AOC) story. According to her biography on the United States House of Representatives website, she was born in the Bronx to a working class Puerto Rican family and at thirty

years old began her campaign for Congress while waiting tables and tending bar. She was elected to Congress in June of 2018. By August 2020, she had more Twitter followers than Nancy Pelosi, then speaker of the house. (Edmonson, 2019) Her social media reach is a benchmark of communications achievements Mercury would be proud of.

AOC was a coauthor of the progressive "Green New Deal," a package of legislation proposed to Congress to address climate change and economic inequity. This highly controversial resolution (which was defeated in the Senate fifty-seven to zero that year) outlined a ten-year economic plan that would phase out fossil fuel use and overhaul the nation's infrastructure.

Mercury is at work in AOC's rise to prominence in several ways. Her ability to be as active as she was on social media early on in her campaign is a Mercury capacity. She has the street cred of a bartender as well as the intellectual capacity for deciphering complicated legislation. Mercury adores that kind of range. She has a knack for graphic and informational design (as evidenced by her campaign materials) as well as for science (she has a minor asteroid named after her in honor of longevity experiments she conducted out of Mt. Sinai Health System in New York). (Mosher, 2018) Versatility like this is also a hallmark of Mercury.

The fact that American politics were influenced by informal social media, previously the sole domain of formal journalism, shows a feature of our collective evolution toward "hive mind." Where journalism is typically one-way (here's all the news you need to know), social media is two-way (here's what

I think, how about you?). By being able to see how our friends weigh in on any given issue, our perception of the matter is swayed, for better or worse.

Over the centuries, decision making has become progressively more decentralized. The "swarming" patterns that social media allows brings that decentralized decision making to a whole new level. Social media is simply training wheels for what is to come. My astrologically informed sense about it is that within our lifetimes, we will be using devices, technologies, platforms, and modes of communication that we cannot even imagine today.

DECOLONIZING OUR MINDS

Just as decentralized processes take control out of the hands of the few and puts control into the hands of the many, decolonizing practices take the centering of certain value systems away from one group, leaving the value systems of the many to operate at will. Newly emerging value systems will have a much better chance of thriving when the destructive and limiting old programs have been nullified.

Author, scholar, and professor Michael Yellowbird is a citizen of the Three Affiliated Tribes: the Mandan, Hidatsa, and Arikara Nations. He works with Tribal and indigenous peoples to bring mindfulness and *neurodecolonization* approaches to these communities for the purposes of healing and improving wellness.

The structures of colonization continue in the Americas, not only in our cultures, but in our bodies and, especially, our brains and nervous systems. Consider the lasting effects for both the colonizer and the colonized to be told that the English language is the only valid one and the lasting effects of erasing indigenous languages, customs, dress, and beliefs through a process of forced assimilation into the dominant culture.

If we are to evolve Mercury collectively, one of our urgent first steps will be to lessen the suffering that continues in all those experiencing the effects of colonization.

Dr. Yellowbird describes decolonization as "activities that weaken the effects of colonialism, facilitate resistance, and create opportunities to promote traditional practices in present-day settings." Neurodecolonization addresses the nervous system, "combining mindfulness approaches with traditional and contemporary secular and sacred contemplative practices to replace negative patterns of thought, emotion, and behavior with healthy, productive ones." (Yellowbird, 2021)

Dr. Yellowbird examines how the stresses of colonialism shape mind and brain function, compromising the well-being of indigenous peoples. Some stressors he examines are racism and hate crimes; loss of territories, culture, and pride; high levels of mortality, poverty, and poor health; and disregard of indigenous Peoples' sovereignty and rights. He explains, "Along with building new empowered neural networks, neurodecolonization activities are aimed at deactivating old, ineffective brain networks that support destructive thoughts, emotions, memories, and behaviors, particularly, past and contemporary oppressions associated with colonialism."

The same destructive worldview that allows one group to colonize another is responsible for human colonization of the Earth. It is an immature stage of collective Mercury development that perpetuates this problematic worldview. Consider this excerpt from a talk by animist Dr. Daniel Foor about a popular worldview he encourages us to examine:

> *There are no environmental problems, really. There are human behavior problems. And it's worth thinking of those behavior problems as arising from the confusion that we are... alone on Earth. And that everyone who isn't human is a thing. And that frame, that very isolating and arrogant frame leads to consent violations, violations of others' space, and well-being. (Foor, 2021)*

The legacy of colonialism and racism is that we have quite a bit of clean-up to do inside our brains and nervous systems. Whether we are currently aware that we are suffering or not, these legacies live inside all of us because they are part of the collective mind. This clean-up is our current evolutionary frontier, our first order of business, where Mercury is concerned.

Writing Prompt

The benefit of undoing structures in our brains and nervous systems is that we free ourselves up to create new worlds that don't replicate the old dysfunctions. What does your ideal world look like?

Write the manifesto for your utopia. Set a timer for ten minutes. You can use this sentence stem to get you started: In my utopia, we believe ____.

FOOD FOR THOUGHT

Clare Fox needed to heal her body. She was accustomed to Pop Tarts and Hot Pockets—microwavable "foods"—but her growing community of social justice peeps started turning her on to nutritious foods at their potluck dinners. She remembers the moment as an adult when she meticulously followed the directions on the back of a bag of Trader Joe's swiss chard, never before having attempted to cook that leafy green. That night she felt the promise of actually liking vegetables, similar to the glimmer of feel-good you might get early on in a dating process. It was a moment of confluence for her, when multiple tributaries of meaningful experience all came together—community, health, vibrancy of mind, and food.

Clare went on to work with, and eventually became, the executive director of the Los Angeles Food Policy Council (LAFPC), a nonprofit that works toward healthy, affordable, fair, and sustainable food for everyone. After ten years with the LAFPC, Clare became the vice president of Strategic Partnerships at Everytable, a private benefit corporation whose mission is "to transform the food system to make delicious, nutritious food accessible to everyone, everywhere." (Everytable, 2021)

Clare recognizes the need for multiple stakeholders to have a say and influence inside our food systems. This itself is Mercury in action, because before the written word was accessible to the general public via the printing press, Mercury's significations were more about commerce, or the currency flows that connect us. Clare is impassioned about strengthening everyone's access to good food through two interconnected flows:

1. Development of robust public food policy. Most utilities are considered public rather than private, including water. We believe in our right to have water. Why not food?
2. Social enterprises that lend capacity and infrastructure to move good food through our food systems to fulfill our right to food.

The shaping of systems is Mercury at work. Clare has devoted her professional life to helping shape our food systems.

My conversation with Clare illuminated something I didn't fully understand about food systems until she spelled it out for me:

> *Food systems are what make food possible in our lives, and some people own and control and have access to it and many, many people do not. They don't have agency or sovereignty within that system and, therefore, do not have access to this thing that is most essential for our lives: food. This is by design.*

Clare explained to me how food systems are used as tools of oppression. Keep people from accessing nutritious food and you vastly limit their potential. When contemplating this through Mercury's vantage point, I began to see how all currency flows—information, money, public resources, reputation, and identity—can either flow freely or get clogged up by human problems, like greed. Before speaking with Clare, I hadn't considered how essential access to food is for a well-functioning Mercury.

"The mind belongs to the body, after all," Clare mused. A well-nourished body is going to have a much better shot at a well-positioned mind than a malnourished body will.

"When we consume plants, we are taking in the intelligence of those life forms," Clare says an old mentor of hers once taught.

Our intelligence, the quality of our mental state, the capacity of our body to produce generative thought, is literally a function of the food we eat.

EVOLUTIONARY COMPETENCIES: WISPS OF MERCURY

If I wrote this book in 1610 when Galileo first asserted the Earth was moving around the Sun, a chapter on Mercury would suggest very different things than what I am about to say. Because we are in the first half of the twenty-first century and have focused on critical, rational, linear thinking for centuries, left brain development, while important, is not where I will suggest Agents of Evolution put their focus.

Instead, the evolutionary movements of Mercury have more to do with the right brain (think: intuition) and the corpus callosum, that thick bundle of nerve fibers that allows the left and right sides of the brain to collaborate. My guess is that we will also discover, in biological terms, something about how humans are *always* broadcasting and communicating, without words entirely.

At this time in human history, Mercury's developments involve not just our rational minds, but the entire process of perception and communication itself.

LISTENING

One of the primary ideas social theorist Otto Scharmer puts forth is that "form follows attention or consciousness. We can change reality by changing the inner place from which we operate." Scharmer, a senior lecturer at the Massachusetts Institute of Technology, explains in his book, *Leading from the Emerging Future,* how this might be done. He proposes an update to our social operating system, "from an obsolete 'ego-system' focused entirely on the well-being of oneself to an eco-system awareness that emphasizes the well-being of the whole." The practices Scharmer offers can help to update and hone our Mercury function.

One of Mercury's abilities we can all develop is our capacity to listen. In *Leading from the Emerging Future,* Scharmer describes the evolution of our listening capacities as they progress through four levels:

1. **Downloading:** This type of listening is limited to reconfirming what we already know. Nothing new penetrates our bubble.
2. **Factual listening:** We let the data talk to us and notice disconfirming information. Doing this requires opening the mind—that is, the capacity to suspend our habits of judgment.
3. **Empathic listening:** We see the situation through the eyes of another. Doing this requires opening the heart:

using our feelings and our heart as an organ of tuning in to another person's view.

4. **Generative listening:** We listen for the highest future possibility to show up while holding a space for something new to be born. (Scharmer, 2013)

Deciding to upgrade our capacity to listen will require strong personal initiative; we are not culturally encouraged to listen in the ways Scharmer describes as higher levels of listening. Most of our listening tends toward what Scharmer refers to as "downloading" or "factual listening." Moving to higher levels, we have all had moments of empathic listening, so this mode of listening is not new, just slightly less common. Generative listening, however, is a highly active, participatory form of listening, and it is quite uncommon. One trick I like to use when practicing generative listening to motivate myself to move through my fear of losing my own position is to approach the conversation from the attitude, "What is the most magical thing that could possibly happen in this conversation?"

Yet, the benefits of higher levels of listening can make the difference between a "you or me" world (the ego-system awareness Scharmer refers to) and a "you and me" world (the eco-system awareness he encourages us to cultivate).

Practice Pause

Call to mind a recent difficult conversation. What level of listening were you operating from? What might have motivated you to move to a higher, more multi-dimensional level of listening?

ALLOWING FOR COMPLEXITY, NOT-KNOWING, UNCERTAINTY

"I mean Negative Capability, that is, when a man is capable of being in uncertainties, mysteries, doubts, without any irritable reaching after fact and reason."

—JOHN KEATS

The Romantic poet John Keats is credited with coming up with the phrase "negative capability." (Keats, 1958) He used it in a letter in 1817 to describe something great writers do. For all of us, negative capability is a Mercury muscle we can develop—tolerating the discomfort of uncertainty.

Defenses arise while listening to others express their viewpoints when we don't like or agree with or understand what they are saying. Their view challenges our own assumptions, which can make us uncomfortable; but we can cultivate the capacity to tolerate that discomfort.

Since the transition moment we are in has us encountering other viewpoints often and confronting all the uncertainty that goes along with that, collective evolution by its nature can throw us headlong into heaps of discomfort. Our destabilized conversations can function as doorways leading to next level mind, nonetheless. In order to be in a state of receptivity rather than reactivity, we might start to cultivate some degree of the negative capability Keats speaks of.

CULTIVATING OTHER WAYS OF KNOWING

Beyond rational, linear ways of knowing, there is a living, pulsing field of wisdom that does not fit through the neat little pathways our left brain loves. Engaging with this field requires a few things:

1. Dropping our insistence on consistency, reliability, and seeming smart.
2. Not caring if our discoveries make sense to others.
3. Not being overly focused on any particular outcome; being willing to stay in process with this changing field forever.

The rewards of learning how to engage with this field are colossal, similar in scope to the advantages gained in moving from crawling to walking. Crawling is not *lesser* than walking, but we do tend to learn how to crawl before we learn how to walk. In learning how to walk we also give up certainties. But that doesn't stop us from learning how to walk. We receive all sorts of assistance from our parents and family to move from crawling to walking. We don't necessarily have that same assistance for this process of dipping into a living field of knowledge. There aren't many examples of this around us. Those of us who pursue this skill are pioneers.

This vast field of knowing surrounds you right now. Can you hear that collectively inherited voice that tells you: "You are crazy for leaving your left brain; you are stupid for thinking you can connect with truth directly; you're ridiculous; you're primitive; you're pathetic," as the crawling one being afraid to walk?

Practice Pause

Set a timer for two minutes.

Close your eyes and use your breath to become present to your body and its surroundings. What does that shimmering, pulsating field have for you right now? Get curious and discover.

A daily practice of sitting meditation provides excellent training wheels for accessing the natural ability you have for other ways of knowing. This is not meditation's ultimate goal, of course; it's just a sweet benefit.

NET ZERO BY 2050?

It will be fascinating to watch Alexandria Ocasio-Cortez's long career unfold in front of the American public. She will no doubt help to shape US politics in ways that keep it on its toes. It seems largely up to her and those her age to bring in the sweeping reforms needed to get us to Net Zero by 2050. (We reach net zero when the amount of greenhouse gas we remove from the atmosphere is equal to the amount we produce. We can achieve net zero by both reducing the carbon dioxide emissions that come mostly from the burning of fossil fuels as well as engaging in actions that create carbon offsets, such as planting trees.)

AOC will be in her sixties in 2050, but she will always have the benefit of having started young—a gift that comes with Mercury's favor.

EVOLVING THE COLLECTIVE MIND

No matter your language—words, music, touch, food, the visual arts—you can develop your capacity to communicate with other humans. Since we each carry the "live," working template of our collective mind, we each have the capacity to change the template for the whole. It's two-way like that. Decentralized. Circular. Non-hierarchical.

Sitting in that concert hall all those years ago, the trumpet player's soaring notes lit a fire in me to communicate what is in me to say. What do you already know is in you to say? How will you say it?

4

VENUS: FALLING IN LOVE WITH US

"Building community is to the collective as spiritual practice is to the individual."

—GRACE LEE BOGGS

POPSICLES AND FIREFLIES

Late in the summer, the sun's heat clung to our small bodies in beads of sweat, especially delicious when zipping through the patch of grass between our neighbor's house and ours. Barefoot, of course, to feel the grass prick my skin as I ran, the movement through the humid Pennsylvania air dragging a pocket of August sky along with me.

My sisters and our friends in our easy summer clothes, hair tangled from so much revelry, playing hide and seek on the block. Surprising squeals from someone in their hiding place, then sprinting so I'm not tagged. Whether I'm chasing or being chased, I like this feeling of my body in motion.

It's our mom's birthday, and the adults are inside, doing whatever mysterious things adults do. One of them brings out popsicles. We hush as we each pick the bright color of sugar water we want. I pick red, of course. It seems to punctuate the freedom of playing outside.

Stripping away the sticky sweet wrapping while droplets fall, already melting in the late afternoon summer heat. Toes on concrete-and-crushed-stone driveway catch some of the drops. A luscious sensation. I see if I can aim a drop from up high at my left big toe. When I miss by a fraction of a margin, I squish the little blob in a satisfying splatter.

We're meandering now, bodies through grass, sugar drunk and happy, as twilight paints the sky in new hues. And that's when the magic really begins. . . little buttons of light dancing in the air. First a few, then many. The yelps come as we chase and catch them. The way the tiny legs feel on my palm as the firefly walks over my hand. This moment of pure enchantment writes itself in my body's memory forever.

Venus's pleasures are a gateway to Love. When we feel good, when our animal bodies fill with well-being, when joy softens our mind's need to protect itself, we have an easier time connecting with others and with the world around us. In that connection lies infinite magic.

THE ASTROLOGICAL VENUS

If there were one planet whose favor has been most pursued since time immemorial, it would undoubtedly be Venus. Style, grace, charm, sensuality, artistry, beauty, popularity, money. Who doesn't want more of the gifts Venus brings?

All the best things in life are Venus.

When Venus is strong in our lives, our relationships, our professions, and our bank accounts thrive. When Venus is challenged, they suffer. We court Venus by appreciating beauty, by valuing refined things, by metaphorically wining and dining our muse, by loving people and being sweet to them. We show Venusian strength whenever we prioritize harmony over independence, or being right, or getting offended.

Venus represents those aspects of our lives in which we feel pleasure. One of Venus's blessings, for instance, is a fine appreciation for the sensual world. Sight, sound, smell, taste, and touch all come alive when Venus is strong in a chart. When someone knows how to slow down enough, has the sensual palate to notice the subtle distinctions between ingredients, and is intuitively able to create pairings that bring pleasure, Venus is at work.

Many of the enjoyments Venus delivers are things we have collectively, culturally defined. Things like what has value, or what we consider to be feminine (or, how we "perform" the feminine gender). Even the concept of aesthetics is Venusian. Fads, trends, fashions, taste—these are domains in which Venus is arbiter.

How we "do" relationships is also a function of Venus energy. Venus helps us harmonize with others in our culture in a way that allows us to understand what the culture values, and then to create beauty, conversations, meals, events, and anything else we would enjoy together.

As complex, multi-dimensional, and intoxicating as any muse, Venus gives her gifts to those artists with whom she is pleased. Prioritize Venus for a spell—through small acts like appreciating beauty, spending time creating a really tasty meal, being polite in an interaction that could just as easily raise your ire, cleaning and honoring all the material resources that surround you and making your life beautiful— and she will bring you sensual delights that seem unearthly in their pleasure.

Sexual attraction and attractiveness belong to both Venus and Mars. While Mars represents the more instinctual, animal sense of attraction we feel with each other (think pheromones), Venus rules over the more culturally defined, emotional, conversational, sensual attraction we have for each other.

Often our norms about what is attractive derive from popular culture, which can cause aesthetic judgments to override a more Martian, body-level magnetism that someone triggers in us. For example, a woman who is physically attracted to one man but chooses to mate with another because of his status is making a Venusian decision.

Regardless of society's outer dance with attraction, each person's individual, private, inner Venus will exert a unique pull. From this inner Venus perspective, beauty truly is in the eye of the beholder. Mathematician Blaise Pascal once famously explained how this inner Venus trumps all logic:

"The heart has its reasons, of which reason knows nothing."
(Pascal, 1877)

Attraction exists between all things in Nature. This is *eros* at work—the Venus principle that creates not only babies, but also great works of art, events we all enjoy, conversations that delight. One of Venus's greatest gifts is "lust for life"—a kind of eros we might experience just for being alive that draws out of us our unique grace and style. Allowing this eros to fill our days, making us artists playing at life, lights up everyone's world.

Just like any Light, Venus too has her shadow sides. The stranglehold of vanity; the tyranny of politeness; niceness or flattery as manipulation; insincerity; superficiality; excessive material focus; excessive attachment or possessiveness— these are the not-so-flattering sides of the goddess of beauty, grace, and charm.

The deeper octaves of Venus relate to being genuinely kind as opposed to being nice. The Dalai Lama's statement, "My religion is kindness," is a Venusian statement. Or the capacity for empathy, rather than simply being polite for harmony's sake. Or the valuing of inherent beauty—the unaltered shapes, dimensions, colors, directions, sounds combinations, textures, flavors, rhythms—found in any given moment, rather than adhering to superficially constructed versions of beauty.

OUR LONELINESS EPIDEMIC

How is it that we in the West are materially richer than ever, but also lonelier than ever?

Dr. Vivek H. Murthy served as the nineteenth Surgeon General of the United States from December 15, 2014, to April 21, 2017. Just as lockdown was beginning here in the States in early 2020, he published *Together*, a book exploring the Venusian theme that we humans are social creatures. *Together* makes a case for loneliness as an alarming public health concern. Dr. Murthy links loneliness to many of the epidemics sweeping our globe, from alcohol and drug addiction to violence to depression and anxiety. Loneliness, he argues, "is affecting not only our health but also how our children experience school, how we perform in the workplace, and the sense of division and polarization in our society."

The main reason one of the foremost authorities on public health in our country is concerned about the loneliness epidemic is its link to a reduction in life span. The effects of loneliness on lifespan are similar to those caused by smoking fifteen cigarettes a day and greater than the impact of obesity. Besides reduction in lifespan, loneliness is associated with a greater risk of heart disease, depression, anxiety, dementia, reductions in task performance, limitations on creativity, and impairment of executive function. (McGregor, 2017)

Maybe we have gotten too caught up in surface expressions of Venus at the expense of her deeper dimensions? Have we perhaps lost connection with ourselves as well, due to the pleasure deadening feedback loop of excessive materialistic inputs?

These questions offer useful avenues of inquiry for the Agent of Evolution.

EVOLVING EROS

Venus's evolutionary path may be the most enjoyable of all. We set out to have more fun, to create more and more magic, and to love ourselves and each other better. When we do this, the goddess of Love cannot help but smile on us. It is her divine nature.

The catch comes when we don't feel worthy of all this goodness. Or when we buy into thoughts or beliefs that pleasure is wrong. Or when we skimp on a creation, stopping short of its full potential (always add extra butter! Or vegan sprinkles—whatever is your Venusian jam!).

Venus's primary path of evolution has to do with learning how to love ourselves so deeply, so lavishly, so totally that each expression of ours is filled with her abundant loveliness. This is how we please Venus.

STAYING IN THE CONVERSATION

I have known Gina Duquenne since 2015, when we worked together at a hospitality company in our little mountain town of Ashland, Oregon. Walking into our marketing office I found Gina's contagiously fun-loving energy genuinely uplifting. That and she always had the sassiest shoes! From her desk, Gina dealt event sales for the many hotels in the hospitality company's portfolio, helping to create some of the most extraordinarily magical weddings and parties in the Rogue Valley. Venus herself would have been delighted.

Gina's story, though, carries an inspiring, deeper vein of Venus. Upon moving here from southern California with her wife, she served a predominantly white, cisgender, heteronor-mative clientele. What you have to know about Gina before I go on is that she could charm anyone into anything. She is one of the most socially gifted human beings I have ever met.

When I asked her, "What's the secret sauce? How can any of us be more charming like you?"

"Just be yourself," she replied.

And this truly is Gina's secret—she genuinely loves people, *and* she's just being herself. It puts everyone at ease, and social scenes flow accordingly.

Gina looked around our small town when she got here and thought to herself, "Where are all the people like me? Where do they hang out? Where do they party?" She came to find out there really weren't any venues, any dedicated events for the LGBTQ community. She also sensed that some people didn't know if it was okay to be public about their love. Ash-land being a town that loves a good parade, Gina decided she would start a PRIDE parade here. At first, it was just a fleeting thought: "What this town needs is a PRIDE event! A celebration of the LGBTQ community that everyone can enjoy." She mentioned the thought in passing to her daughter, and her daughter nudged her, "Mom, why don't *you* start it?"

It took two years to get from initial thought to inaugural parade—to get the permits, to talk to the shops on Main Street, to raise the support and financial backing to pay City Hall the parade fee, and maybe even to gather up the courage. Her biggest success, however, was winning over the shop owners who initially refused to put up signs for the parade. During the first parade, she passed a couple of those shops and saw they had made their own signs and put them up in their windows.

How did she win them over? I had to ask. "I just kept talking," she explains, "I stayed in the conversation." She put the shop owners at ease through conversation. She was the same outstanding event planner they had all known and loved so well. None of that changed because of her relationship choices. She drew on a deep understanding of Venus to allow them to come around.

The joy this parade surfaces in our town to this day no longer belongs to just the LGBTQ community. Like any event where we celebrate as one community—Cinco de Mayo, Holi Festival, Mardi Gras, Christmas—we have a chance to celebrate us all, in all our diversity.

Last year, Gina won a seat on the City Council. She's the first Black person to serve there. No doubt she'll keep on winning over the hearts and minds of locals in this valley on a variety of issues. Venus works like this—she cajoles, she seduces, she enchants, she charms, all while being herself and staying in the conversations and connections she so enjoys.

FALL IN LOVE WITH WHAT LIGHTS YOU UP
Nina Simons is an international speaker, leadership author, and educator, as well as social entrepreneur who is passionate about the power of women to transform the world. She cofounded Bioneers and serves as its chief relationship

strategist. Nina's work includes racial and gender justice, indigeneity and rekindling a sacred relationship to nature, and cocreating a just transition that's regenerative, loving, and peaceful. At the center of everything she does are the themes of women, embodied practice, leading from the heart, and relational intelligence—Venus themes, through and through.

From the introduction to her book *Nature, Culture & the Sacred: A Woman Listens for Leadership*, Nina embraces a Venusian orientation toward solving the world's problems—she encourages us to fall in love:

> *I suggest that you first give yourself permission to fall in love. Fall in love with. . . anything that really lights you up. Then give yourself to it in some sort of purposeful action. You don't have to know what that means, exactly, or have it strategically mapped out in advance. You just have to commit to being its ally, to acting to defend or protect or improve its life. Then see who else is committed to it.. . . Bring all of yourself. Lastly, I suggest that you trust that exactly who you are is what is needed at this moment in the world and that you are enough in every way to meet this assignment. Here's the best part: I'd suggest you do this not because it's right (though it is), not because it's needed (though it surely is), but because it is the most joyful, purposeful, and fulfilling way to live your life.*

Nina spoke to me about a specific way of being in a relationship that communicates one of the inner strengths of Venus practice. She mentioned how she strives to stay present even when a conversation is making her uncomfortable.

"If we are willing to give focus, time, and love to practicing this, along with real commitment," she says, "we can evolve through a lot of messy growing pains to be able to work together in a new and regenerative way."

Once at a Cultivating Women's Leadership retreat in rural northern New Mexico, Nina and the retreat co-facilitator explored the collective pain of racial wounding with the participants. On the last night of the retreat, Nina was awakened at three o'clock in the morning. One of the women participants was gasping for breath from an asthma attack. She had forgotten to bring her inhaler. Nina saw the terror in this woman's eyes.

Nina's mind had no context for what was taking place, so she turned to the wisdom of her body. Asking the woman's permission, she held her head against her chest. She breathed slowly and deeply, stroked her head, and began rocking while humming something like a lullaby without words.

The woman of color having the asthma attack was an environmental justice leader, and the conversation about race from earlier in the day may have triggered the response her body was now having of not being able to breathe.

"I don't have any illusion that I healed her," Nina says. "But thankfully, after what seemed an endless time, her breathing steadied and slowed. As she calmed, I laid her head back down on the pillows. I sat beside her, stroking her head and face. When she'd closed her eyes, and was breathing normally, I sank down to the floor beside her bed. Tears were streaming down my cheeks."

Nina knew the shell of her separateness had cracked open:

> *The barrier that my privilege had created between my head and heart had been pierced. I felt the pain of this woman's asthma and the profound injustice of her having to live with it acutely. I knew it was caused due to racial bias, redlining, and corporate greed and malfeasance, and my heart ached even as my anger was kindled to change it. In that instant, I also knew my own complicity and accountability for it. No matter how many years I'd known about the most toxic industries being sited in poor inner-city neighborhoods, and the suffering that results from the toxic inequities, corruption, and corporate abuses of our current systems, no matter how long I'd known about the elevated rates of asthma and diabetes, of heart disease and cancer in these communities, I had known them from the distance my privilege afforded me. I had known them as statistics that shocked and saddened me, but I had never before felt the direct impacts of that injustice the way I did so personally that night. (Simons 2019, 174–176)*

The collective barrier that our privilege has created between our heads and our hearts melts one relationship at a time. Any time any of us has an experience like Nina's, we step closer to a much more beautiful, collective world.

Practice Pause

Can you feel the barrier that your privilege has created between your head and your heart? If it had a shape, what shape would it be? Does it have a texture? A color? Does it make any sounds? What is it fond of saying? Where does it live in your body? Take a minute to be with the feelings that arise as you contemplate this. Make a silent prayer to Venus to help gently melt away that barrier at a speed that she knows will be comfortable for you.

EVOLUTIONARY COMPETENCIES: PETALS OF VENUS

Evolution is cyclical rather than linear. Venus's evolutionary movement is a case in point. At the present point in our collective evolutionary cycle, we are not in need of an *upgrade* to Venus so much as a *return* to older Venus wisdom. We have gone a little too far afield where Venus is concerned, grasping at her self-oriented gifts (wants—like money or comfort) while completely ignoring other, more fundamental, communal wealth (needs—like the well-being of all people or the Earth).

The following evolutionary movements all fall under Venusian skies. When the goddess of Love reigns, beauty soothes our tensions and we invoke harmony and cooperation to solve our collective problems.

RELATIONSHIP, BROADENED

For too long, "relationship" in the Western world has been defined in narrow, binary ways. The available options are: familial love, romantic love between a man and a woman, or friendship. Anything else is suspect. But at this stage in human history, Venus encourages us to celebrate others in loving the way they choose, so long as consent is given before their exchange.

We might also begin to examine the way we limit our sense of relationship to the human realm. We are constantly in relationship with everything around us. To live in this way is to hear the higher octaves of Venus. The more than human world—rivers, the wind, nature spirits, homes, trees, to name a few—is constantly in relationship with us as well, whether we want to recognize it or not.

All relationships require tending. Once we realize all the ways in which we are constantly in relationship, we must tend them, *out of love*.

TENDING THE COMMONS

Venus asks us to tend not just the people we are engaged with, but also our chosen sites for assembling. The concept of reciprocity with the land is found in many indigenous traditions. Reciprocity is more than "you do something for me, and I will do something for you." When we tend any relationship out of love, including the relationship with place, with land, it is a joy to give back.

The *Commons* can refer to a public beach, software code, community gardens, decentralized, alternative currencies, or even clean air. Anything that is a benefit to us all can be held as a "Commons." One Venusian evolutionary development is reengaging with this web of interdependence.

In an essay titled, "The Commons as a Template for Transformation," David Bollier spells out how we might employ the Commons mindset:

*In the face of the deep pathologies of neoliberal capital-
ism, the commons paradigm can help us imagine and
implement a transition to new decentralized systems of
provisioning and democratic governance. . . [The Com-
mons] can give participating members a significant degree
of sovereignty and control over important elements of
their everyday lives. They also help people reconnect to
nature and to each other, set limits on resource exploita-
tion, and internalize the "negative externalities" so often
associated with market behavior. These more equitable,
ecologically responsible, and decentralized ways of meeting basic needs represent a promising new paradigm for
escaping the pathologies of the Market/State order and
constructing an ecologically sustainable alternative.*

Beginning to wrap our minds around how we collaborate
over our shared resources will help us focus not just on what
we can take from the land, but also on what we can give.

As we practice reciprocity throughout all our Commons,
we come to recognize that another's well-being promotes
our own heart's best interest. When we shut off this natural
function of the human heart, we really get ourselves into
emotional heartache. (It would be like blood entering the
heart through the veins but the arteries blocking the flow of
blood to the rest of the body.) Although being focused on my
own individual desires to the exclusion of yours can seem
fulfilling for a while, it is ultimately lonely and depressing.
We are just not wired to be eight billion little islands with our
own TVs and lawnmowers. We are designed to share: meals,
memories, knowledge, pleasure, conversation, life, love.

REEXAMINING VALUE AND AESTHETIC

Venus is sensual. If we want pleasure and delight to be part of our world going forward, we will want to align with where Venus is heading. This requires tending not only to people and places, but also to the "things" of this world—all the objects we make and enjoy, like clothing, homes, jewelry, art, vehicles, meals, and more.

Current economic models link scarce supply to profit for some. That's one way to rig the game. What if instead we linked abundant supply to the benefit of all? For instance, what if instead of valuing a scarce supply like oil, we valued abundant, renewable energy resources like solar and wind? This is not a new concept, but somehow our Venusian sensibilities still haven't caught on. My sense is it has to do with aesthetics.

Once we make this shift in values, new aesthetics surface based on the new design parameters. Electric cars look and feel different than gas powered cars. We would collective arrive at a new aesthetic as soon as we give our Venusian designers permission to play with the new values. As more of us align with a set of values that benefits all of us (including the Earth), we will coerce shifts in aesthetics, which will in turn force shifts in commerce and industry.

Here in the US, defending and promoting these values will largely be up to all who identify as female, given that women control the lion's share of consumer spending. (Davis, 2019) As it should be, since values, money, commerce, and aesthetics are all Venus's domain.

Writing Prompt

Venus wants us to feel good. To approach any of Venus's evolutionary goals, we'll want to start with what brings us joy. Try the following writing prompts in the order suggested to remind yourself that evolving Venus does not require giving up what you love. On the contrary, a collectively oriented Venus gets us closer to what really makes our hearts happy, delighted, and fulfilled.

First:

Write about **the life you dream of living**, five years from now. Sketch a visual representation of this dream life—it could be a drawing, a diagram, a bunch of words floating on the page, a cartoon. . . Draw an iconic form of your visual representation on a Sticky note and put it on your laptop. Realize that you are creating a blueprint for the universe to build from—so let your enthusiasm bubble up! Venus is magnetized by your enthusiasm.

Second:

Write about **the world you dream of inhabiting**, five years from now. Sketch a visual representation of this world. Draw an iconic form of that world on a Sticky note and put it next to your personal life dream icon Sticky note on your laptop. Feel the relationship between them every time you look.

MORE VALUABLE THAN GOLD

"Many more of us now are seeking clarity for how best to develop ourselves to protect and defend what we love. We're heeding a call to act on behalf of a future where diversity in all its forms is valued for the strength and resilience it can offer, and life's creatures and living systems can thrive along with our kids and grandchildren."

—NINA SIMONS

Without prioritizing our web of relationships with each other and the natural world, we fall apart at the seams. In our pursuit of greater material comfort, we might become materially wealthier, but we become isolated, disconnected from the natural world and each other. We stop feeling pleasure.

To renew our capacity for pleasure, we must heed the call of our own heart. Our hearts know we can't put a price on Venusian gifts we collectively value and love (like clean air, clean water, the lands our ancestors tended). It's absurd. And dangerous.

START WITH LOVE

Fireflies will always bring me the pure pleasure of childhood. I adore the mountains and grand vistas of the West. But I do miss thunderstorms and fireflies—two things my Pennsylvania childhood had in abundance.

While with some planets our evolutionary journeys require wholly new developments, with Venus we are in need of recapturing some of the older, simpler, more advanced ways we have lost touch with.

You can start with calling to heart who and what you are in love with. Who and what and where makes your heart melt and your pleasure centers light up? Begin by tending those relationships. Any other way of starting puts the cart before the horse.

5

MARS: A NEW COURAGE

"Wage Love."

—CHARITY HICKS

SKYWALKERS

With three thousand feet between him and the Yosemite Valley floor, he walked a thin, wiggly ribbon in the sky. Tears streamed down my face as I watched—was this emotion or the howling wind beating at my cheeks? Could have been either. The blue sky felt thinner up here, empty and vibrant at the same time. Every cell of my body tingled. No thoughts needed. An experience, complete in itself. The euphoria of the scene was almost unbearable.

The sport of highlining began innocently enough as "slacklining." In slacklining, a person walks on a strip of maybe two-inch-wide nylon webbing strung above the ground between two points but not stretched tight. Not falling off requires incredible balance. Highlining negotiates that same slack nylon line rigged high in the sky, often thousands of feet above the earth.

A large group of us had backpacked into this hallowed spot of slackline history—the Lost Arrow Spire—to celebrate the life of one of the original highliners. The irony of the highliner's death was that at age fifty-five, a car accident had taken him to the beyond, not one of his many "sends" of this very line without a safety harness. (A send is when a highliner makes it across and back without falling off the line.)

I was filming the event for a documentary I was making and felt privileged to be witnessing the current generation of slackliners taking the activity to altogether new heights. Most of these young men between the ages of seventeen and twenty-five felt like old Souls to me, with more wisdom among them than many three times their age. The eight or so young men walking the three lines that had been set up, and the five or so older men helping them, had worked the entire day rigging the lines in preparation for this moment. The rigging itself was a majestic feat, a testament to our human capacity for achieving impossible things.

And now, the pre-sunset light painted the ancient landscape in ever changing hues. I wondered whether this was the experience of the Soul after death.

The whipping wind made it difficult to hear each other, so there wasn't much talking. But no words were needed to communicate the tight knit between this band of humans. It was clear they put complete trust in each other's skill and rallied each other's "stoke."

The seventeen-year-old now summoned our united attention as he stepped onto the swaying line, surfing the gusts of wind. The

safety harness he wore as protection from falling did not lessen my
breathlessness. I imagine it did not lessen his body's instinctive
fear response to doing something bodies don't usually do—walk
thousands of feet in the air with nothing solid beneath. Fear or
not, he walked. Standing there watching, I felt my own body soar.

Fear and exhilaration were hard to distinguish as I watched
him walk out from the safety of primordial granite at the edge
of heaven, observing this feat of human imagination, skill,
courage, athleticism, and achievement.

This indomitable spirit embodies the gift of Mars.

THE ASTROLOGICAL MARS

Though Mars expresses himself most directly through the
body, Mars energy can be found in all domains of life. In a
soup, Mars would be the pepper. Mars is what gives anything its kick. The trick with Mars is to be able to regulate
the intensity, the strength with which his energy circulates.
Too much Mars can easily destroy any situation. Too little
and the situation deflates, becomes uninteresting or boring,
or never even gets off the ground.

Mars fuels forward motion, progress.

Without what Mars represents, humans would not evolve. We
would be content to be as we are, without any urge to improve
our condition. Mars represents that impulse that gets us out
of bed in the morning, gives us the mojo to exercise, motivates us to learn new things, to create more resources for
everyone, and to leave the world better than we found it.

We are at a time in human history, however, when the expression of Mars has become painfully distorted. With "toxic masculinity" on the rise—needing to dominate for ego's sake, appearing to have no needs, showing no emotion, and needing to win at all costs—everyone loses. Mars is so much more dimensional than just force, strength, domination. Mars represents that instinctual urge within us that arises from our mammalian brain to connect with others in sports-like ways, enjoying games and human rituals that mark for us our progress or excellence, and the structures we organize around, which tell us what is worthy of defense and protection.

Mars is that movement in us that tells us when an important line has been crossed. And Mars also represents the movement to protect boundaries. Taken to the extreme, Mars rules all militaristic activities. In Roman mythology, Mars was the god of War. The term "martial art" derives from Latin and means the arts of Mars.

In traditional Vedic medical astrology, Mars rules the blood. Vedic medical astrology accompanies another ancient wisdom tradition that derived from Indian Vedic culture, the healing system known as *Ayurveda*. (Lad, 2006) The Vedic birth chart is read by Ayurvedic practitioners to offer insight into a patient's physical makeup. The flow of our blood is a distinctly Mars phenomenon. Our heart muscle, with its pumping action, is the command center of a vast intricate system of blood vessels, distributing blood and all the resources that it carries, such as oxygen, all over the body. Without the blood, nothing functions. This runs in perfect parallel to how Mars distributes energy throughout our life.

EVOLVING PROGRESS

"If you realize that all things change, there is nothing you will try to hold on to. If you are not afraid of dying, there is nothing you cannot achieve."

—LAO TZU

The evolutionary path of Mars requires us to learn a certain kind of warriorship of spirit. With a warrior's honor and integrity, we won't let ourselves off the hook with sloppy, haphazard showing up. We show up with full presence and attention and honesty. We protect what gives us life.

DIRECTING BIG YANG

Learning to channel this big yang energy in useful pursuits, though, puts us up against all our pettiness. We discover all the ways we give up, complain, blame, or direct anger wrongheadedly. The evolutionary path of Mars involves learning how to navigate conflict, mistrust, and frustration and learning how to channel our own aggression, passion, jealousy, and the urge to dominate.

In cultures like ours, where the passions are allowed to run amok, we don't always notice that not skillfully directing Mars energy leads to senseless violence, loss on all sides, and an increasing feeling of powerlessness or impotence that must always be fed with *more* violence and domination. Maybe for this reason, much older cultures like those in East Asia have a spiritual component to martial arts training that centers the maturity of Mars—martial energy in relaxation, at the total command of a centered mind and a grounded nervous system, rooted in an emotional wisdom that comes with control of the senses.

YIELDING

"He who conquers himself is the mightiest warrior."

—CONFUCIUS

The Mars path of evolution requires becoming incredibly astute about your own body. Not everyone will be an athlete, but Mars benefits from studying the body's movements and patterns and flows, where things get stuck, where things erupt, where things pool, where they exit. Knowing the body can help to funnel all our life energy, or "Chi," in productive ways.

Different movement forms have been employed by many civilizations throughout time—movement forms from East Asia like Qigong, (pronounced Chi•gung,) or yogic asana practice from India—that help practitioners work with their own body's energy. Newer movement forms have sprung up here in the West as well, many of them based in part on these older forms.

Mariko Tanabe is a practitioner and teacher of one such newer system called Body-Mind Centering, developed by Bonnie Bainbridge Cohen. Mariko and I have studied together in various communities of self-development practice. I have often been struck by a quality of effortlessness and relaxation that Mariko brings to group spaces, the way she "embodies" poise inside stressful or tense situations.

When I asked Mariko how she keeps her equanimity with the group even when things get hard, and not do what I usually do which is tighten and clam up, she told me about a Body-Mind Centering practice called "yielding."

In yielding, you essentially *open to a state of "non-doing."* You allow yourself to stop defending yourself from gravity. You give yourself fully to the Earth. You yield your mass to what is beneath you, and in doing so you find that relationship, in the moment, between self and gravity, between self and the environment.

Yielding differs from collapsing. Bonnie Bainbridge Cohen explains that in yielding, there is actually a spontaneous increase of tone on the side of you that is in contact with something other than space.

"When we collapse, we lose contact. When we give up, we let gravity take over and then we are collapsed. But when we respond by feeling this increase in tone, it will support our rising away from the Earth. There's a rebound." (Bainbridge Cohen)

This rebound is what I witnessed Mariko embodying in group settings. As a dancer and choreographer, Mariko *knew* Bainbridge Cohen's tone principle so well in her body that it translated into her life and relationships. Whether on the dance floor or on a Zoom call, she was able to move into moments of tension and maintain contact by becoming present with herself and leaning in. Instead of collapse or destruction, there was rebound, fresh energy, new possibility.

She says, "When we yield, our hearts can soften, our blood can flow to better guide our actions."

Mariko remembers a moment when she received a profound teaching about yielding. Many years into the planning of a project, she felt the original plan for the project was no longer working. She was conflicted about what to do and turned to Bonnie, who was mentoring her at the time. Bonnie simply put her fingertips on Mariko's chest, ever so gently, and said: "Just yield, Mariko.... Just yield...." and after a long pause, "then you will know what you truly need to do."

Mariko's way of being in the world fundamentally changed after this gift from her teacher.

Practicing various movement forms over years also helps develop our body's capacity to withstand the arising of stronger Mars emotions like fear, or anger, or competitiveness, or jealousy, or even contempt. These emotions course through the body and create physiological shifts. Having trust in the body to tolerate the discomfort strong emotions bring goes a long way toward not reacting in ways we'll regret later. Being able to sit with discomfort allows us to move through the trauma responses of fight, flight, and freeze, and instead access the calm and balance essential for staying present.

When we start to become aware of energy patterns in our bodies over a period of years, in moments of anxiety, distress, or conflict, we become capable of adjusting the flow of our energy for a positive net effect on the situation.

Practice Pause

Call to mind a current conflict in your personal life that is giving you a bit of grief. Imagine the person causing you stress standing in front of you. Feel the conflict between you. Where does it live in your body? Does it have a shape? A color? An age? A texture?

Lightly place your fingertips on your chest and hold them there for fifteen seconds. Say to yourself, "I yield." Allow the energy from your intention to yield flow through your fingertips, into your heart, through your blood vessels, and to the part of your body where that conflict lives. Feel this place in you receiving the gift of your own evolution.

Do not confuse yielding with collapse. Just because you yield within your own heart does not mean your outer actions toward the one you are in conflict with will necessarily change. Your inner stance, though, will shift. See if it brings you a bit of peace.

GIVE MARS A WORTHY GOAL

"Of all the dangers we face, from climate chaos to nuclear war, none is so great as the deadening of our response."

—JOANNA MACY

We've covered the glories of Mars. Now let's look at his shadow. Mars's shadow is easy to spot in others and a little harder to notice in ourselves. It is usually painfully evident when Mars has gotten out of line. Like a fire that's out of control, Mars bullies and destroys. This makes Mars a challenging energy to wield skillfully.

Mars motivates both the destructive terrorist and the heroic firefighter. In order for Mars to shine in our twenty-first century lives, we have to give Mars a worthy goal, one that honors our interconnectedness with all of life. This is one of the main elements that distinguishes a badly acting Mars from one whose courage is behaving honorably—a worthy, collective-centered goal, rather than a competitive, self-centered goal, or a fear-based reaction.

In our relatively young country here in the United States, the dominant culture worships Mars and the excesses of his immature expression: domination, aggression, impatience, taking whatever is wanted without consent or thought of the whole. A problematic Mars is behind most of the violence that runs rampant here in the United States. A more mature and self-aware Mars might look to elders for how to channel all that energy.

Just as the transition from youth to elder in an individual has its challenges, cultures transitioning from young expressions to elder expressions are also challenged. You might say we in the United States are adolescent in our craving for Mars-style excitement and are challenged to know what to do with our "fighting spirit."

What is needed at this present stage in our journey is Mars's mature capacity to turn the direction of Mars's "gaze," the term the ancient yogic seers used to describe a planet's direction of influence. We need to shift from looking outward to looking inward.

Can we, as a culture, direct the same energy and passion we would typically put into winning and dominating and growth, an outwardly directed Mars, to becoming more grounded, more centered, more self-aware, an inwardly directed Mars? How do we do that?

One of our own elders here in the United States, eco-philosopher Joanna Macy, is among the first to refer to the age we are in as "the Great Turning." She defines it as "the essential adventure of our time: the shift from the industrial growth society to a life-sustaining civilization." (Macy, 2009) Navigating the Great Turning well is a collective goal worthy of a more collectively mature Mars.

There are no guarantees, of course, that we will make it through this collective growing-up phase. Who hasn't done something reckless in that delicate rite of passage into young adulthood? I certainly did foolish things that could have easily cost me my life. Cultures and collectives have no guarantees, either. But the maturation process must go on, replete with the inevitable growing pains.

Writing Prompt

Take a minute and consider Joanna Macy's call to action—shifting from an industrial growth society to a life-sustaining civilization. How do you recruit

your fighting spirit toward this worthy goal? Complete this sentence stem to find out:

If I were able to marshal all the energy available to me, the one thing I would do for the sake of my world is _____.

(This writing prompt is borrowed from Joanna Macy. She introduces "open sentences" like this one in her workshops as a form of group practice. For more on Joanna Macy, and for more on practicing with open sentences, please visit the Resources section and Notes in the back.)

EVOLUTIONARY COMPETENCIES: MARS'S DOJO

The word "dojo" means "the place of the Way" in Japanese. Dojos are spaces where students immerse themselves in learning martial arts. For an Agent of Evolution, the world is their dojo. Every interaction with another can be a place for practice. Luckily, Mars likes to practice. His focus is laser-like, so he progresses quickly with practice.

That same focus and intensity, though, gets Mars into trouble. Like a dog with a bone, our instinctual Mars becomes possessive of people, or places, or ideals, or states, or any number of things and defends our right to possess them. Our animal instinct is to exert dominance in the situation.

Channeled differently, that laser-like focus—Mars's capacity for getting in the zone—can give us a seemingly superhuman ability to act impeccably in situations without having to think about what we're doing. Direct knowing takes over, a kind of effortless, full-bodied awareness of the most elegant movement through the situation. Take, for instance, someone pulling their child back onto the curb so they aren't hit by a passing car. No thought required—just pure, effective action.

Imagine turning that zone state inward, toward ourselves and our own evolution, perceiving the truth of who we are with that same relaxed but heightened awareness. This is a skillful use of Mars energy.

What follows are pathways or skills through which to cultivate Mars's maturation. One individual maturing in this way sets off a domino effect of ripening in their communities. Countries mature as their citizens do.

THE RIGHT USE OF RISK

"The steps we take can be modest ones, but they should involve some risk to our mental and social comfort lest we remain caught in old, safe limits. Courage is a great teacher and bringer of joy."

—JOANNA MACY

Risk, when taken to benefit ourselves, is like consuming empty calories. That kind of risk may yield the desired result, but it has no meaning. Only in recognizing our place in the web of life does our risk-taking become meaningful. Risk taken on behalf of the greater good flexes Mars's muscles.

For instance, I might risk my reputation by writing a book I know some will ridicule. Since I take this risk knowing in my heart of hearts it may help some readers gain perspective and give them hope, I take the risk on behalf of the greater good. If, instead, I take this same risk simply to get noticed, there's a good chance the whole endeavor will ultimately feel meaningless. When I enlist Mars to work on behalf of the web of life, I infuse all my actions with meaning.

FEAR? SO WHAT

"Courage is not the absence of fear. It is the ability to act in the presence of fear."

—BRUCE LEE

"Careful you must be when sensing the future, Anakin! The fear of loss is a path to the Dark Side. . . Rejoice for those around us who transform into the Force. . . Train yourself to let go of everything you fear to lose."

—YODA IN REVENGE OF THE SITH

When Mars energy is motivated by unconscious fear, it creates destruction. When Mars energy is aware of its own fear, and motivated by Love and Wisdom, there is no more powerful force in the world.

The so-called courage of the terrorist bent on destroying an enemy, real or imagined, might bring short-term gratification but solves nothing in the long term for the terrorizer. The courage of a father, on the other hand, rushing into a burning building to save his child promotes life. The terrorist may think they work on behalf of a higher ideal, but any trace of a fear motivation sets them up for an escalation in offensive measures down the road. The goal someone is working toward must be an all-inclusive goal in which all of life has its place. Any defense of elitism or exclusion will incorporate fear into its structures.

The body's fear response to threat is completely instinctual. Although tricks may exist to short-circuit fear, the only way to *evolve* this reptilian response is to cultivate an awareness of fear and its movements and grow the ability to tolerate discomfort to evaluate whether a threat is real and the level of response it requires. It is a day-to-day, living practice of studying every detail about how fear moves inside the body. With fear acknowledged and worked with in any situation, a potent, new set of possibilities exists.

LIBERATING CONFLICT

For some of us, conflict is a dirty word. For others, conflict is liberating. Some of us avoid conflict at all costs. Some of us crave the drama and are drawn to it like moths to flame. Some of us are somewhere in between, lucky to be able to pick it up and put it down when necessary. Conflict can destroy, but it can also release energy, show a new way through, and heal. Working with conflict is an inescapable part of Mars's path of evolution.

Working with conflict, in ourselves, in relationship, in community, in social justice movements, requires heaps of self-awareness, skill, practice, resource, and self-compassion. It takes time to hear the voice of your own cruelty as an internalized message from the past. Only as this awareness dawns can we wield Mars skillfully. Conflict without cruelty can be an awe-inspiring social dance. Many individuals shaping our social justice movements have Mars strong in their birth charts. We can turn to the ones we admire to learn about navigating conflict.

Author, social justice facilitator, Black feminist, and doula adrienne maree brown is one strong example of finely honed Mars energy. In her books, she artfully describes the new kinds of courage and skill we need to move through the social change at our doorstep.

Brown has rich insights on holding space for conflict in a generative rather than destructive way. Her book, *Holding Change: The Way of Emergent Strategy Facilitation and Mediation*, describes mediation as "an ancient human practice that happens in intimate space." She speaks about the lineage of facilitators she comes from: "The way I walk with whispers of Harriet Tubman, Fanny Lou Hamer, Ella Baker in my spine, how I feel guided and driven forward by their bold legacies."

Showing how we can weave past with present to strengthen the capacity to work with conflict, brown credits several Black feminist colleagues for shaping her as a facilitator and conflict mediator. "I have done most of my mediating around a kitchen table, over tea, where people can see and feel each other. I imagine a lineage at my back, of oak trees and mycelium and grandparents, knowing this moment is temporary and survivable," she says. Our body tells us something is survivable, which is why daily movement practice is helpful. Without practice, the body resorts to fear ruts. It takes practice to avoid those ruts and stay present to what is happening in a moment of conflict.

She shares a further wisdom about working with conflict: "Mediation holds that the current moment is not the only moment, and that there are things we can do to decrease harm and increase respect and communication over time to change conditions and dynamics."

Spiritual liberation can be found by taking any of the planetary paths *all the way.* Taking Mars's path all the way is about liberating conflict.

THE HUMAN FRONTIER IS WHEREVER YOU ARE

That night at the Lost Arrow Spire, I couldn't sleep. Luckily my bivy shelter allowed me full view of the starry night, there atop the granite slab in Yosemite. The air had a cleansing quality, as if it had the magical power to erase every care or worry that had ever visited me. All my senses were alive with what I had witnessed that day. I didn't want the moment to end. This feeling is what I had been after my whole life, but I didn't know it until then.

With the group of us who had convened for the weekend snoring in their nooks along the span of crag that was our encampment, I made a vow to myself to always, always feel this alive. I looked up at Mars, bright in the sky that night, and he seemed to wink in response to my intention.

Mars does not guarantee success, but he does guarantee progress for the Soul. Enduring failure and not have it crush you, as well as experiencing honor and realizing the emptiness of that as well, is part of training in Mars's dojo. You can't fake detachment, for it is a bodily experience. But you can, and must, practice knowing and working with the patterns and flows of all the body's instinctual drives.

When you feel like every cell of your body is wide awake and alive, know that Mars is offering you the path of valor.

PART III:

SOCIAL PLANETS

Jupiter and Saturn
Spiraling form
Arouse and commit us
To our human bloom

Jupiter and Saturn are classified as social planets because they show us trends in how we assemble in groups for collective benefit—groups like families, communities, businesses, organizations, nations, religions or spiritualities, and social movements.

These two titans reflect our collective values, organizing ideologies, and resulting structures. With Jupiter's orbit around the solar system lasting twelve years and Saturn's lasting roughly twenty-eight years, both planets reflect wider changes in the culture that take longer periods of time to unfold.

PART II

SOCIAL PLANETS?

6

JUPITER:
THE WEB OF GIFTS

———

"Dissents speak to a future age. It's not simply to say, 'My colleagues are wrong and I would do it this way.' But the greatest dissents do become court opinions and gradually over time their views become the dominant view. So that's the dissenter's hope: that they are writing not for today, but for tomorrow."

—RUTH BADER GINSBURG

A BRUSH WITH GREATNESS

It is a good thing I knew I was lucky. Otherwise, I may have taken working at National Geographic headquarters in Washington, DC, for granted. During a time when magazine publishing had much more formative impact on the mind of the nation than it does today, I was learning photojournalism from the best of the best, and I knew it.

A cadre of top brass magazine staff filled the small, warmly lit gallery room. Devoid of any furniture, save the light tables where photographic transparencies could be viewed, the focus of the room was what hung on the walls. As a production coordinator in the magazine's Layout and Design division during my early twenties, it was my job to hang the stories for the "wall walks," during which this editorial team decided the fate of stories.

I listened as the editors, photographers, layout designers, and writers commented on the story on the wall before them. The air in the room was pregnant with tension like the moments before a thundershower. Wall walks strung months, sometimes years of a journalist's life on the line as stories got either accepted, chopped up, sent back for do-overs, or canned. The editorial group at the wall walks considered each carefully selected photograph within the story's narrative arc, making delicate decisions about how scientific discoveries and far-flung places would be represented to the magazine's loyal readership.

As the group filed out the door, the editor of the magazine hung back to take one last look at the story on the wall. I was usually the last to leave, hoping to let the group's gift for visual narratives sink into my aspiring storyteller's bones. (I may have also had talent crushes on every single one of those photojournalism greats.)

"What do you think?" he asked me when he realized someone was still there in the room with him.

Stunned to be asked but also clear about my opinion, I pointed to the layout sequence I preferred. "This one flows better," I offered.

"Hm. [Another long pause.] Good work getting this up there for us with the tight timeline," he said as he tapped on the doorframe on his way out.

The swoon that happened after he left may have been one of the top five fangirl moments of my life.

The *National Geographic Magazine* (*NGM*) and the National Geographic Society (NGS) it grew out of are Jupiter-style institutions, through and through. Privilege, prestige, and the pursuit of knowledge are all Jupiter's dominion. Before the internet, *NGM* stories were a defining voice for the American people, a primary viewfinder on other cultures, the natural sciences, and the natural world.

Jupiter also represents well-established education and research institutions, the culturally defining canon they produce and further, and the endowments that fund them. The National Geographic Society is a great example of this. In 1888, a group of academics interested in travel and exploration plus some well-to-do patrons willing to fund their ventures founded the National Geographic Society. (Wallace 2007) Early on, inventor of the telephone Alexander Graham Bell served as the Society's president. (Evans, 2011) The Society's contributions in science, exploration, education, and storytelling have all the magnitude, heft, and scope of Jupiter; their reputation for expertise in these matters is Jupiterian to the core.

THE ASTROLOGICAL JUPITER

Generosity, cheerfulness, privilege, prestige, gratitude, luck, good judgment, magnanimity, largess (and largeness!), expertise, teaching, law, arrogance, entitlement, faith, belief, philanthropy, the elite, and a jovial disposition. These are some of the key identifiers that astrologers associate with astrological Jupiter.

Jupiter represents our faith in the goodness of life.

When Jupiter (a.k.a. "the planet of good luck") is strong in a chart, we tend to be sailing our ship through enviable seas. We are born into the right circumstances that can support the full development of our gifts. When Jupiter is challenged, either *natively* (at birth) or by *transit* (current astrological influences), we can tend toward a lack of faith. A condition of doubt arises, sometimes in a situation or in relationship with another person, but most often within ourselves. A challenging *aspect* to Jupiter can make us doubt that any benevolence is present in the universe at all. This unfortunately has the effect of closing us off to the expansion that Jupiter wants to bring.

We all know that feeling of being in flow, where everything is humming along nicely, the world loves us, and all the serendipities line up to greet us with bright smiles. This kind of attitude is magnetic and draws more opportunity, more positive people, and all manner of expansion into our lives. Jupiter's influence often comes in the form of "candy grace": all the good experiences that life gives us freely for which we have done no work at. In other words, those experiences that feel like pure good luck.

When we experience gratitude for such lucky turns, we directly contact the majesty of Jupiter. Activating our awareness and appreciation of Jupiter's power and presence brings what we want directly to our doorstep. This appreciation begets magnanimity, which begets cheerfulness, which begets more abundance in a cycle of good feeling and positive experience that just keeps growing.

In his classic text *The Astrology of the Seers*, Dr. David Frawley describes the wondrousness of Jupiter:

> *Jupiter is well known as the most helpful, generous, and benefic of the planets. His grace has always been sought by the votaries of astrology. In Sanskrit, he is called Guru, "the spiritual teacher" or "guide." He signifies dharma, the law of our inner nature, which is the law of creative evolution and self-realization. He shows our principles in life, our guiding light of truth.. . . He is the planet that indicates such domains of principle as law, religion, and philosophy. He is a spiritual and ethical planet which insists upon the pursuit and support of the good. He establishes our good in life and through his influence that goodness comes to us.*

The challenging side of Jupiter comes along when we don't recognize when enough is enough. Maybe we get greedy or start expecting all the good things with a sense of entitlement. Or maybe we start thinking all those good things are coming to us because we are inherently worthier than others to receive them. Maybe we have an inflated sense of our abilities or our worth, or an unexamined sense of superiority because of our privilege. Or maybe we become overly optimistic, not planning enough for contingencies. Maybe we start taking more than we need or more than we give. When the gas giant gets too full of himself, life yanks us back to Earth, helping deflate a little air from our overblown balloon.

JUPITER'S SHADOW

On the collective level, institutions are challenged to stay nimble as they grow. This applies to both tangible institutions, like the *National Geographic*, or abstract practices or customs, like the institution of marriage. The institution may begin with noble intentions. But growth of an institution—a Jupiter-ruled development—often brings with it the entrenched, unquestioned attitudes of an elite group. The institution of marriage, for instance, centers heteronormative values.

The *National Geographic Magazine* (*NGM*), despite their noble intentions of research and exploration, centered whiteness. It operated from an unchallenged assumption of hierarchy, with the English-speaking, Western world at the top of the hierarchy, and Black and Brown people below them. (Wamsley, 2018) It wasn't until the year 2018 that the *NGM* acknowledged their racist past, in their April 2018 publication devoted to "The Race Issue." (NGM, 2018)

In a self-conducted audit enlisting the help of John Edwin Mason, a professor of African history and the history of photography at the University of Virginia, the *NGM* reckoned with their "long tradition" of racist choices in text, subjects, and photography. Pictures of people from other cultures in particular objectified those cultures, not giving a voice to those people being represented. The depiction of bare breasted women for which they became notorious in the fifties and sixties were always women of color. The Black and Brown world was presented as primitive, backward, and generally unchanging. (Wamsley, 2018)

NGM Editor in Chief Susan Goldberg avowed, "How we present race matters. [It] means we have a duty, in every story, to present accurate and authentic depictions—a duty heightened when we cover fraught issues such as race." (Wamsley, 2018) This is a step in the right direction in an institution noticing its own Jupiter shadow.

Current leadership of many elite institutions like the *National Geographic* may or may not be ready and willing to contend with their Jupiter shadow. Yet contend with this shadow we all must. Institutions today are challenged to continue to examine their own ethics as they grow in prominence and must find ways to more equitably and humbly share their privilege.

Despite the many possible pitfalls, Jupiter is without a doubt *the* planet in the chart you want to have as your ally. Collectively, once we tune in to deeper dimensions of Jupiter, we might very naturally discover the solutions to course correct, because Jupiter is the ultimate arbiter of our ethic, pointing the way forward.

EVOLVING POSSIBILITY
Observing astrological cycles over many years allows a student of the stars to gain unshakeable faith in our sine wave style development—first we go up, then we go down, then

up again; this, then that; yin, then yang; in, then out. Very little in nature goes forward in one direction forever without doubling back or reversing direction. This is especially true of Jupiter.

Our human presence on Earth has gone in one direction for a very long time. Our dominant operating system of endless growth has now expanded beyond what the Earth can sustain. The Global Footprint Network explains:

> The world's ecological deficit is referred to as global ecological overshoot. Since the 1970s, humanity has been in ecological overshoot, with annual demand on resources exceeding Earth's biocapacity. Today humanity uses the equivalent of 1.6 Earths to provide the resources we use and absorb our waste. This means it now takes the Earth one year and eight months to regenerate what we use in a year. We use more ecological resources and services than nature can regenerate through overfishing, overharvesting forests, and emitting more carbon dioxide into the atmosphere than forests can sequester.

This overshoot is a classic Jupiter cycle shift point, reflecting the need for us to understand how much is enough; to restore the honor of sustainable, right-sized exchange with each other and the Earth; and to cultivate contentment by simplifying our lifestyles.

Jupiter always brings expansion. But that expansion has to be supported by every dimension of the system. So, when further expansion in one direction isn't possible (i.e. material, outer expansion), then Jupiter forges a new path for us in a different direction. In the twenty-first century, Jupiter has reached a pinnacle of outward, material expansion in the Western world. His trajectory of expansion now must travel in a different direction—*in*.

GIFTS IN CIRCULATION

All the lucky things in life—that big break in the career, winning the lottery, or getting just the right kind of help exactly when you need it—are attributed to astrological Jupiter. What if instead of thinking of those things, that wealth, as random *luck*, we understood them to be *gifts carrying the seeds of greater growth*?

This nuanced adjustment in our way of stewarding the resources given to us is key to Jupiter's path of evolution. By choosing to see goodness that comes unbidden as a gift, not only do we connect to a kind of benevolence the system is endowed with (when we choose to see it that way), we also start to own our part in the interrelatedness of all things. Seeing resources as gifts may even prevent us from getting too big for our britches (a distinct Jupiter possibility) when we stop hoarding because we realize that gifts are meant to be paid forward.

In his book, *Sacred Economics*, Charles Eisenstein points out how money, once a token of gratitude, has become so divorced from this original concept that this benevolent, intrinsic potential of the web of human relationships suffers. He explains: "It is ironic indeed that money, originally a means of connecting gifts with needs, originally an outgrowth of a sacred gift economy, is now precisely what blocks the blossoming of our desire to give, keeping us in deadening jobs out of economic necessity, and forestalling our most generous impulses with the words, 'I can't afford to do that.'" Money has become the master instead of serving the gift economy.

We speak of the "cost of living." What a strange notion. Eisenstein points out, "Our purpose for being—the development and full expression of our gifts—is mortgaged to the demands of money to making a living, to surviving, yet no one, no matter how wealthy, secure, or comfortable, can ever feel fulfilled in a life where those gifts remain latent. Even the best paid job, if it does not engage our gifts, soon feels deadening and we think, 'I was not put here on Earth to do this.'" I would say about a fourth of my clients find me when they are getting ready to change out of jobs that pay well but suck the life out of them. When we do not give our gifts, we wither.

Jupiter's evolution within us requires us to return to this understanding of all of life as a divine gift. When we do this, we also understand ourselves to be connected to that web of life, and therefore we become inspired to give of ourselves. Eisenstein says, "Our gifts are sacred and therefore meant for a sacred purpose." When we develop that Jupiterian sense of faith and optimism in the benevolence at the heart of human existence, we learn to relax into the intelligence inherent in the system. There is value in each of our gifts. The absence of any one of our individual gifts creates imbalance in the overall system.

Since one of Jupiter's gifts is Faith, Jupiter has been associated with religion throughout the millennia. Today it is as if we feel we have only two possibilities—either the universe is random and uncaring and therefore science wins, or the universe is purposeful and benevolent and therefore religion wins.

Yet, Eisenstein describes a possible hybrid third space as a real possibility in apprehending an inherent truth of the natural world: "One can make [the argument] that the view of biology as consisting of myriad discrete separate competing selves—organisms or 'selfish genes'—is more a projection of our present day culture than it is an accurate understanding of nature. There are other ways of understanding nature that, while not ignoring its obvious competition, give primacy to cooperation, symbiosis, and the merging of organisms into larger wholes. This new understanding is actually quite ancient, echoing the indigenous understanding of nature as a web of gifts." Science wins, *and* the universe is benevolent.

Do we want to view the glass as half empty (nature as competitive) or half full (nature as collaborative, nature as a web of gifts, the universe as benevolent)? What do you think Jupiter would say?

Writing Prompt

If I lived in a world where all my basic needs were met by the world around me, what gift would I be free to offer the world?

YOU'RE WELCOME

Pertula says her mother taught her, "I'm not better than anyone, and nobody's better than me." Respect and inclusion were living practices in her household, where family members come from a variety of socioeconomic backgrounds with some experiencing poverty, some who are in and out of prison, and others who are highly educated professionals. She credits the culture she grew up in, in Saint Lucia, for the ease with which she relates to everyone. In Pertula's presence, I feel elevated. I can feel her radiant self-respect and the way it invites me into a whole other exalted way of relating. I feel the blessings of Jupiter both in how she holds herself and in how she holds me.

Having grown up in a predominantly Black country and being the descendant of slaves, Pertula has been motivated by her connection to the Black community to work toward the vision that all people are humans regardless of their skin color and should be treated with dignity and respect.

In September 2018 in Dallas, Texas, Botham Shem Jean, a relative of Pertula's, was fatally shot in his own apartment by his neighbor, an off-duty Dallas police officer. It was a tragic experience for Jean's family. Then, after George Floyd was murdered in 2020, Pertula was lit on fire to take action. With a Master's Degree in Sustainable International Development and over a decade of social justice work already under her belt, she did some intensive Soul-searching into what the hurting Black American community needed and how she might respond.

During her nonprofit career in the field of sustainable agriculture, Pertula had been told, "African Americans are not interested in farming because of the stigma of slavery." So, she began researching the plight of the Black farmer and discovered, as she told me, "[Black farmers] have lost millions of acres of land through theft and discrimination. Blatant theft. The United States Department of Agriculture (USDA) and lending institutions have robbed Black farmers of their land. In 1920, there were over nine hundred forty-five thousand Black farmers, and today there are roughly forty-five thousand. Not solely because they're not interested in farming but because of racism and theft. As of today, there are farmers who are losing land because of discriminatory practices. It's systemic racism."

Pertula pinpointed the need—Black farmer's access to land—and decided to fill it. That's how Acres4Change was born. The organization's mission, as Pertula described, is to create economic stability through land ownership, professional development, and racial healing. The non-profit organization accomplishes this goal through acquiring land (via land donations, tax sale purchases, and outright purchases from capital grants) and putting it in the hands of people who have been discriminated against, giving them legal rights or access to the land.

Acres4Change does not stop there, though. The organization recognizes that legal rights to land are not enough for the success of Black farmers. That is why they also sponsor professional development and racial healing practices that support land recipients to be successful at the business of farming. Pertula explains that "a big component is therapy and racial healing for folks who have experienced trauma by [having to endure] racism."

In reaching out to her network of associates, Pertula discovered that often, Black farmers who are graduating programs and are ready to farm have no access to land. Pertula set about enlisting several experts and key players to work with her to remedy this. Support began coming in from every-where. The University of Baltimore provided all their legal services pro bono; master of public health students from Cornell University assisted the organization with grant writing; and Virginia State University, University of Maryland Eastern Shore, Farm Alliance of Baltimore, Future Harvest, and the Black Yield Institute are all considering running the pilot program through their Beginning Farmer Training programs. Since its inception in July of 2020, the project has taken on a life of its own, and Pertula recognizes she is just along for the ride.

With the kind of skills Pertula possesses, she could easily have gone into more lucrative work. I asked her what motivates her to do work in which she prioritizes giving back over her own personal gain. She explained that in the Caribbean culture she came from, it is ingrained that you give back. She recognizes her experience in, knowledge about, and success with real estate and development can help others learn and benefit.

"I will be content when other people, whether they're family members or not, are also doing better. When individual lives improve, the whole society benefits."

Perhaps what is thought of as "philanthropy" in the United States is just a natural way of life for some cultures. When Pertula returns to her father's house in Saint Lucia, the front door is always wide open. Anyone can, and does, come in at any time. Pertula describes Caribbean culture as generally warm, welcoming, and community oriented. Neighbors look out for each other in a real way. They recognize no one can do it on their own, and they don't try to. To a large extent, grandparents live with their families rather than in retirement homes. They all have a hand in raising the young ones. Their fabric of community is strong. They are a model for Jupiterian "welcome."

Practice Pause

Close your eyes and take a few deep, long, slow breaths. Call to mind a person who is always there for you, always your biggest fan, someone who always has your best interest in mind. (This could also be a pet, or a tree, or a place.) Feel what it feels like to be in this person's presence. Notice what their "Welcome" feels like in your body. Send their welcome all over your body, feeling each part of your body relax.

Next, come up with a gesture you might do with your fingers to remind you of this feeling (e.g., tapping the inside of your left wrist with your right ring finger, putting your right palm over your heart, or tugging on an earlobe).

The next time you find yourself in a situation where you feel unwelcomed, bring this resource state of welcome back by repeating the gesture. Consider this gesture Jupiter's talisman for you.

HARBINGER OF HOPE

With a focus on making the whole of human experience a prosperous, expansive one, Jupiter's domains include philanthropy; higher education; religions and spirituality and higher truth in general; and law.

Why is law included in this list? It is easy to see how philanthropy supports everyone being prosperous. It is easy to see how higher education expands our view. Seeing how faith in a higher truth, no matter what we believe in, brings us meaning, purpose, and, to many, expansiveness is easy. But law?

I propose to you that the purpose of law, whether manmade or observed (like the "laws" of physics, or even the "laws" of astrology), is to describe the mechanisms by which the system the law applies to stays in balance and in a state of equilibrium. Deviating from the law throws the system out of balance. This is one reason why law is included in Jupiter's camp—the law promotes human prosperity by defining its balance.

Imbalance, by definition, benefits some parts of the system and not others. Imbalance is an indication of Jupiter gone rogue. The bloated conditions which result are a tip-off to the otherwise invisible imbalance. Law is an attempt to correct that imbalance, to restore equilibrium.

The United States is in a condition of massive imbalance, financially, ethically, educationally, and culturally. One US civil rights attorney working toward restoring balance is Vanita Gupta.

Gupta has an impressive civil rights legal resume. Before being appointed United States Associate Attorney General, Gupta, the daughter of immigrants from India, was the president and chief executive of the Leadership Conference on Civil and Human Rights, an organization whose motto is: "Building an America as good as its ideals." She has been victorious in key civil rights cases, including securing a settlement on the behalf of immigrant children that led to the end of "family detention" practices at a Texas facility. (Hewitt, 2021) Gupta has aggressively prosecuted discrimination and injustice on many fronts—racial, gender, and disability discrimination, and labor injustice, to name a few. Some of the cases she has worked on involve situations so contentious and hateful, I wonder how she gets any sleep at night.

The ace in her pocket seems to be Hope, and this is where Gupta can serve as a model for those on Jupiter's path of evolution to consider, since Jupiter traffics in Hope. In a lecture she gave at Brandeis University in March 2018, Vanita Gupta stated, "I firmly believe hope is a discipline. It's a muscle that we have to exercise." Gupta has needed a vast reservoir of hope to work for an America as good as its ideals. She warns us that "our nation's progress has not been guaranteed. And it never will be.... Our values, our Constitution, our democracy, they don't protect themselves. Instead, our progress has really been as a result of people pushing, sometimes inside government, but many, many times outside, on the streets, on our campuses, in our classrooms, in the courts, in the ballot box and in the media.... Each generation must decide for itself that the cause of justice and equality is worth fighting for."

Fresh out of law school, twenty-six-year-old Gupta landed work with the the NAACP Legal Defense and Education Fund looking into a series of cases in the small town of Tulia, Texas. In 1999, forty African Americans were rounded up in the early hours of the morning and charged with dealing cocaine. Virtually all of them were convicted by all-white juries, doling out sentences as high as ninety-nine years. Gupta and her team's investigations found that these convictions were based on the work of one notoriously unreliable undercover officer, shoddy records, and the flimsiest of evidence. That undercover officer was even named Texas Lawman of the Year. (Blakeslee, 2006) Gupta began fighting these questionable convictions, both in the courts and in the media. Finally, in the summer of 2003, after many of the defendants had already spent four years in jail, Gupta won the legal battle. The convictions were reversed, and she negotiated a $6 million settlement for the defendants.

After this victory, Gupta admits she knew Tulia was merely a drop in the bucket of the broader, systemic challenges that defendants were facing around the country. It was with this humbling realization that she learned something interesting about Hope: "Although it can feel like it comes from nowhere and nothing, it grows. There's momentum to hope. There's a kind of multiplying effect that really can't be explained. It's powerful."

EVOLUTIONARY COMPETENCIES: JUPITERIAN BLING

How do we individually remove ourselves from extractive economies? How do we stop viewing all our relations from the vantage point of what they can do for us and begin seeing ourselves as participating in a web of gifts? Jupiter's path of evolution requires us to develop a kind of social intelligence that might take the rest of our lives to unpack. What follows are some signposts along the way.

THE WEB OF GIFTS

The primary capacity we develop on Jupiter's path of evolution is to operate from a restored sense of nature as a web of gifts. This is not easy in the Western world, where we have been programmed into a survival-of-the-fittest, competitive thinking that warns us, "you don't get something for nothing," and "you get what you pay for." Charge that cynical paradigm with destroying life's balance. Interrogate it at every turn with your best inner Jupiterian prosecuting attorney: "What if it actually *is* a gift?"

Charles Eisenstein encourages us to question whether this cut-throat, competitive economy is natural. In his book he posits: "It is an aberration, a peculiar though necessary phase that has reached its extreme is now giving way to a new one. In nature, headlong, gross, and all-out competition are features of immature ecosystems, followed by complex interdependence, symbiosis, cooperation, and the cycling of resources."

In its place, he puts forth this vision: "The next stage of human economy will parallel what we are beginning to understand about nature. It will call forth the gifts of each of us. It will emphasize cooperation over competition. It will encourage circulation over hoarding, and it will be cyclical, not linear."

INTERROGATING PREVAILING EPISTEMOLOGIES

Astrological Jupiter has been associated with "higher truth" for at least five thousand years. (Frawley, 1994) Since Jupiter is one of the brightest lights in the night sky, it makes sense that ancient cultures would associate Jupiter's illumination with knowledge.

At this time in human history, we have again pursued the elementary significations of the planet in one direction for quite some time now. All that is considered valid, useful, justified knowledge tends to lean in the direction of "rational," meaning it employs reason or logic. There are many things worth knowing that do not adhere to rules of logic, yet these things are tragically banished from the Western canon.

We can remedy this tragedy of omission by loosening the ligatures on what we view as valid ways of knowing. When a way of knowing something rings true, investigate it according to its own laws rather than the laws of the prevailing epistemology. For instance, if it makes sense to you that nature is a web of gifts, investigate this web of gifts from within its own laws rather than judging it against the Darwinian notion of survival of the fittest.

CIRCULATING PRIVILEGE

An additional core Jupiter ability we stumble upon if we are lucky is the ability to circulate privilege. Privilege comes in many forms (material, educational status, the ability to travel, career position, proximity to influential people, and so on). All these forms are ascribed to astrological Jupiter. On its own, privilege is a wonderful thing. The problem with privilege—like with many a good thing—is that when it is hoarded or left out of circulation, it pools and stagnates, suffocating itself.

I consider circulating privilege to be connecting someone with something they need that you have an abundance of. This can be done by elevating other people's voices or by philanthropic giving, for instance. By circulating privilege, we honor one of Jupiter's greatest functions: widespread distribution and abundance for everyone.

KNOWLEDGE IS POWER

So much about photojournalism has changed since the 1990s, when I worked at the *National Geographic Magazine*. Digital photography, smartphones, the internet, and social media have done for journalism what the Gutenberg press did for reading. By disseminating access to news and information, technology takes the power out of the hands of a small, elite group of people to decide what news is "fit to print" and put that power into the hands of the common citizen. Jupiter is always looking for ways to send his blessings out along his web of gifts.

Regardless of the change in distribution methods, storytelling itself hasn't changed. We have been telling each other stories since time immemorial. I am grateful for the time I spent at *NGM* learning the craft from master storytellers. Gratitude is quite possibly the best response when Jupiter's gifts come to you. Stay in gratitude and you have a much better chance of your life staying in balance.

WINTER SOLSTICE 2020

At the Winter Solstice in the year 2020, the planets Jupiter and Saturn met in the sky in a dazzling twilight show. Many astrologers believe Jupiter put us on notice that he was about to modify our social contracts, our governing structures, our local and global communities, and all our cherished institutions. Rather than continue to grow in ways that imbalance the human organism and the Earth on which we depend, he would start taking cues from Saturn, the master of consolidation. For instance, rather than promote fossil fuels and short-term profits for some, the United States government has begun to set forth provisions for renewable energy development on public lands. (Congress, 2020)

Since the winter solstice of 2020, and until Jupiter and Saturn meet again in another twenty years in 2040, the set of possibilities Jupiter represents is heading in a different direction. Each one of us can search out the ways and means whereby we live inside his web of gifts.

7

SATURN:
BEFRIENDING TIME

"The only time we suffer is when we believe a thought that argues with what is."

—BYRON KATIE

A DATE WITH DESTINY

I had escaped within an inch of my will to live. Anyone who has been in a toxic, codependent relationship with a narcissist would have recognized in me the telltale signs of trouble: all the days spent believing the gaslighting; being obsessed with winning his approval; constantly being thrown under the bus and believing I deserved his emotional abuse; catering to his wild mood swings and demands. I was a junkie, and he was my drug. My addiction to being around him had rendered me hollow. What in me had allowed me to agree to this self-sabotage?

For months I was held in the thrall of his intoxicating charm, which helped me gloss over the obvious facts—his violent outbursts, a strange dance we began where I allowed him control over my behavior, my thoughts, my values, my interests, my friendships. Was I stupid? Was I weak? This self-loathing helped fuel a last-gasp effort at maintaining the whole intoxicating illusion, but it was crumbling down around me fast. I was losing work, losing money, losing friendships, losing self-respect. I was dissociated, not fully in my body. I got into a car accident in which I rear-ended another car, and the driver I hit sued. My body was falling apart at the seams—an ankle injury wasn't healing, a stomach ulcer was rearing its head, and sleeplessness was beginning to set in. I remember walking around feeling like a ghost, two-dimensional, like I was in a movie.

This had been my first foray into dating after an amicable divorce. In hindsight, I did not understand how grief about my divorce was expressing itself as an obsession with relationships. The new guy seemed to fill the agonizing void. Though I already knew within three months of dating that the connection with the new guy was destructive for me, it took me a solid year and a half to make a successful exit. I was unsuccessful in enforcing my boundaries. It was a twisted game we played where I would attempt to put up a boundary and he would find a way to cross it and then burn it behind him. I tried to end the relationship but kept getting back together with him anytime he came around, until one day I finally didn't anymore. I spent years regaining the life force I lost in the short span of time of that relationship.

It took this shock to the system to cure me of my addiction to relationship. From age nineteen until age fifty, I had never *been single for longer than a couple months. I thought I needed a relationship to be happy. I was terrified of being alone. I leaned too hard on partners to give me things I needed to develope myself, like my sense of my own value or groundedness. That toxic relationship was one of my biggest teachers in this lifetime. Not a teacher I would wish on anyone, but one I value.*

This is the greatness of Saturn: life experiences that bring us to our knees, whether we can see the karmic link or not. If we manage to stay out of self-pity and blame and instead ask, "What development is in this for me?" then we will be rising to Saturn's challenge. Saturn's reward for our efforts? More responsibility, harder work, steeper challenges, and, over time, a deep well of character.

Saturn's lessons often feel harsh, unfair, or even cruel. With Saturn lessons, the point is to find the will and inner dignity to carry on, which requires developing an unshakeable acceptance of our own significance.

THE ASTROLOGICAL SATURN

As old as the hills, as wise as time, as firm as bone, Saturn teaches us things we can only know through lived experience. How does an elder embody patience and endurance and fortitude and humility? The many moons they have lived through developed those qualities in them through a process of weathering. Each day, they got out of bed in the cold and put on clothes in the darkness, which helped them put another brick in the structures they were creating. Each time they recognized a need present in their family and compromised their own comfort to provide for that need, their ability to respond developed. Anytime their life afforded them the opportunity to take a quick and easy, but perhaps ethically questionable, way out and they instead chose the slow slog through right relations, another grain of sand on the beach of character formed.

Saturn is linked to our mastery of Time and Place.

We don't live forever, and we can't be everywhere at once. By observing the limitations on time and place, we master these dimensions.

Saturn is the loner, the stoic, the bachelor, the homeless person; the wise sage with the flowing beard, an ugly crone, a faithful servant; an obstacle, a responsibility, a handicap; a worker, a gardener, a prison guard; a tax bill, a restraint, a stay at home order, a joyless marriage, a somber funeral; an unforgiving lover, a harsh word, a stern father, a cold stare, a painful rejection, a bewildering abandonment; the relentless duties and sleeplessness of a new parent, a librarian shushing people; a speeding ticket, the dry and cracked desert floor, the camping trip when it rains; the prudent decision, the servant leader; the Earth growing over a cottage in the woods, the humorless but excellent math teacher; the cautionary tale; braces, bridges, roads, casts, scaffolding, and graves.

Saturn's gifts don't come easily. They come through time, commitment, showing up—even, or especially when, we don't feel like it and taking whatever life gives us with gratitude, cultivating from it something functional and lasting. The things Saturn tells us we must do are usually things we don't want to do, at least not until we develop enough Saturnian discipline to actually enjoy the process. Which does happen the more you embrace Saturn's lessons.

Internationally renowned astrologer Liz Greene, in her classic text *Saturn: A New Look at An Old Devil*, describes the inner dimensions of Saturn in this way:

> *Saturn symbolizes a psychic process as well as a quality or kind of experience. He is not merely a representative of pain, restriction, and discipline. He is also a symbol of the psychic process natural to all human beings, by which an individual may utilize the experiences of pain, restriction, and discipline, as a means for greater consciousness and fulfillment.*

Saturn is serious, dedicated, tedious, and sometimes boring. He is about efficiency, so he has no time for small talk. He is stark, stern, harsh, and the pain he inflicts can make us self-absorbed. His fingerprints are all over adversity, rejection, failure, bad luck, isolation, and loneliness. Befriending Saturn gives us patience, endurance, humility, acceptance, wisdom, fortitude, maturity, discipline, a hard work ethic, character, and dignity.

Problems with Saturn can come from life itself: an unfair boss, an abusive parent, or maybe a country's tyrannical dictator. Or they can come from our own immature development: not planning for a rainy day; not taking the needs of the whole into account; or pushing beyond our capacity, authority, or resources.

Problems with Saturn in the chart can be one of two things:

1. A difficult circumstance arising from our own immaturity requiring some painful aspect of growing up.
2. An unfair or extreme circumstance arising from intergenerational or collective trauma limiting our ability to be who we are.

Regardless of which type of problem the Saturn circumstance is, it is imperative to move out of blame. This does not mean we push aside discernment about what happened. We can be crystal clear when someone's actions toward us are out of line, feeling all the feelings that brings up, and even demanding accountability, while still having a taproot going down to the beneficence at the core of All That Is.

The goal is not to never land in darkness. The goal is to always be able to return to light. Saturn gives us the will to survive and the skill to do so.

Saturn is gravely misunderstood. Being cautious about seeking out his influence is wise, but it shows misunderstanding to revile him. He works for the greater good in all the most unsexy but necessary ways, at a more productive rate than any other planet. Without Saturn anchoring us inside our human bodies, our spirits would be unable to play here on planet Earth. Saturn is what puts our skin in the game.

As wonderful as Jupiter is, Jupiter can be all hot air, whereas Saturn is down to Earth, practical, applied. Without Saturn, nothing ever materializes. Anyone wanting to accomplish anything in real world terms will want to get friendly with

Saturn. Saturn gives us a kind of natural authority that others recognize. We all respect a person who walks their talk. This is Saturn in action.

Saturn truly is the ace in our pocket. We just don't always enjoy his methods.

THE WAKE-UP CALL

The lights were dim in his office, presumably for all the people he saw for whom bright lights triggered unwanted brain sequences. Every part of my body scrambled to catch up with the new information the doctor was telling me. It was May 2019 when I finally found out about TBI, traumatic brain injury, and how it alters the brain. And there I was, looking at expensive scans printed on a copier, ink freshly drying, a curious smell like fingernail polish remover, while the doctor explained the extent of the damage.

I previously had four concussions during my lifetime that went unaddressed. Like most people in the first world in the late twentieth century, I thought hitting your head was no big deal. It happened all the time, after all. But new medical research was finally making the link between traumatic brain injury and thinking and processing problems, mood disorders, and other body degenerations.

"We'll want to work with medications or supplements—your choice—and nutrition and living habits, as well as therapeutic approaches," the doctor explained as he gave me the official diagnosis of PTSD, depression, and anxiety.

On the one hand, I was relieved someone had the training to show me pictures of my brain and could advise me on how to move forward. On the other hand, there was no pretending anymore that I might solve my crumbling life by just being more positive or doing more yoga. This condition would worsen considerably over time if I didn't address it and do everything in my power to slow or possibly reverse the brain degeneration.

In the course of a lifetime, we get some Wake-Up Calls. This one really got my attention. Life changed with great force after that trip to the doctor's office. I began paying meticulous attention to the food I ate and began an intimidating daily supplement schedule that still feels like a part-time job. I became religious about sleep patterns, sleep hygiene, screen time, energy hygiene, calming environments, and lifestyle. I began rounds of costly and time-consuming physical and behavioral treatments. Certain environments like loud, crowded places would forever bring up the tendency in me to "bonk"—which to others looks like me freaking out, and to me feels like needing to make it all stop.

Wake-Up Calls never come at a convenient time. I had to reconsider the film I was then making, knowing I could no longer sustain the lifestyle it required. I had spent two years fully immersed in the project. It was just beginning to gain some steam. But it was clear I would need to hand it over to another director to complete the project. In that sense, the news was crushing. In another sense, the news was a relief, solving the mystery of why my life kept crumbling in certain ways, no matter my best intentions.

EVOLVING MANIFESTATION

Painful Saturn lessons can be the ones in which a certain amount of necessary fortitude is cultivated for the Soul growth we came to Earth to experience. Without it, we walk the Earth as children, expecting things to happen without putting in our own effort, blaming others when things go wrong, relying on Jupiter to save the day.

Saturn is a taskmaster-style teacher. Failure is the tool in Saturn's toolkit that brings some of our greatest maturity. If at first we don't succeed, try, try again. Saturn likes it when we chip away at things. Failure can teach us humility, right-sizing us in a way no success can.

Saturn's path of evolution is a mountain climb. It takes perseverance, tolerance for pain, a willingness to keep trying after setbacks, an unshakable commitment, and clarity about our true limits. The climbers who push past their *true* limits are the dead ones.

As a culture, we like to believe we can do anything we want, but Saturn would argue, "You *do* have limits." We slowly develop the Soul muscle to take on marginally more, to do marginally more, to accomplish marginally more, constantly expanding our limits and sometimes surprising ourselves with our newfound capacities. A mountain climber would have it no other way. The summit is a reward, but it pales in comparison to the glorious process of getting there.

WEATHERING UNPOPULARITY

Though the glories of Saturn usually come with age, Saturn can be seen working through young climate activist Greta Thunberg. "How dare you," she admonished delegates during her speech at the United Nations in September 2019, when she was just sixteen. (United Nations, 2019) "You have stolen my dreams and my childhood with your empty words. . . People are suffering. People are dying. Entire ecosystems are collapsing. We are in the beginning of a mass extinction, and all you can talk about is the money and fairy tales of eternal economic growth. How dare you!"

The emotional address sent chills through me when I heard it then and still sends chills through me every time I remember it. Greta is right. "For more than thirty years the science has been crystal clear. How dare you continue to look away and come here saying that you're doing enough when the politics and solutions needed are still nowhere in sight? You say you hear us and that you understand the urgency, but no matter how sad and angry I am I do not want to believe that, because if you really understood the situation and still kept on failing to act, then you would be evil. And that I refuse to believe." She expresses with a moral authority only someone of her generation can, since that generation will be the first to shoulder most of the burdens of climate change in their lifetimes.

It takes a willingness to not be liked, to be misunderstood, to be reviled in order to consciously wield Saturn energy. Pointing out a failure, a misstep, bad judgment, incompetence, or calling for accountability is never a popular stance. And yet without the voice of Saturn, no standards would exist at all, and lawlessness would prevail.

BIOMIMICRY

"The forest teaches us enoughness."

—VANDANA SHIVA

Biomimicry is a design approach to which Saturn would give high marks. Design solutions that align with the limitations of the natural world are an intuitively obvious way to please the Lord of Matter.

According to the Biomimicry Institute, biomimicry is "a practice that learns from and mimics the strategies found in nature to solve human design challenges," emphasizing regenerative solutions. Some exciting examples of biomimicry that the institute features on their website include learning from mantis shrimp to make more durable materials; learning from coral to create colorful textiles; and learning from termites how to create sustainable buildings.

Nature abundantly illustrates the democracy inherent in diversity. In a May 2019 article she wrote for *Yes! Magazine*, author and eco-activist Vandana Shiva says, "The forests are sources of water and the storehouses of a biodiversity that can teach us the lessons of democracy—of leaving space for others while drawing sustenance from the common web of life."

Shiva is possibly best known for her global activism around defending biodiversity and the many varieties of seed she has collected and now maintains in a seed bank at her Navdanya Farm. She speaks about how "the forest is a unity in its diversity," and how we can learn from that. "It is this unity in diversity that is the basis of both ecological sustainability and democracy. Diversity without unity becomes the source of conflict and contest. Unity without diversity becomes the ground for external control. This is true of both nature and culture."

"Earth Democracy" is a principle Shiva teaches, which she defines as "the freedom for all species to evolve within the web of life, and the freedom and responsibility of humans, as members of the Earth family, to recognize, protect, and respect the right of other species." This quintessentially Saturnian ethos requires us to stop thinking in a human-centered way and to start understanding our place in the ecosphere.

We can also learn from the forest about how to live within our means and in cooperation with all of life: "No species in a forest appropriates the share of another species. Every species sustains itself in cooperation with others. The end of consumerism and accumulation is the beginning of the joy of living."

This kind of joyful, voluntary simplicity is the pinnacle of Saturnian aspiration.

WHO GETS TO MATTER?

Just as the forest has self-correcting mechanisms for imbalances, human culture has self-correcting mechanisms to restore resilience.

Patrisse Cullors, cofounder of the "Black Lives Matter" movement, is part of a long lineage of civil rights activists working toward racial justice. On her website she asks Saturn's questions: "What is the impact of not being valued? How do you measure the loss of what a human being does not receive?"

Patrisse is a force of nature. I had the pleasure of speaking with her in 2013, right before she became the historic, international figure she is in our world today. She was unassuming, sincere, besieged by grief about her disabled brother behind bars, in a prison system that was an extension of Jim Crow, itself an extension of slavery. Patrisse was looking for answers while creating them at the same time.

In 2013, a phrase she posted on Twitter went viral: "Black Lives Matter." She and Alicia Garzia then cofounded a movement that went on to command attention, both here in the US and abroad. This is the power of Saturn at work.

From the introduction to her book, *When They Call You A Terrorist: A Black Lives Matter Memoir*, Patrisse describes the power of Saturn when she says, "Dr. Neil deGrasse Tyson... is saying that we human beings are literally made out of stardust... I have seen it, since I was a child, the magic, the Star Dust we are, in the lives of the people I come from... I am the thirteenth generation progeny of a people who survived the hulls of slave ships, survived the chains, the whips, the months laying in their own shit and piss. The human beings legislated as not human beings who watched their names, their languages, their goddesses and gods, the arc of their dances and beats of their songs, the majesty of their dreams, their very families snatched up and stolen, disassembled, and discarded." These are happenings only Saturn would have the stomach to survive.

But survival is not Saturn's only goal. When we survive Saturn-style events, Saturn infuses our lives with purpose. Patrisse continues, "And despite [all that we survived, we] built language and honored God and created movement and upheld love. What could they be but stardust, these people who refused to die, who refused to accept the idea that their lives did not matter, that their children's lives did not matter?" When we survive Saturn-style events, we wake up to our own magic.

Whereas belonging, an archetypal Moon concern, is detected as an interpersonal feeling, mattering is detected as an existential fact—an archetypal Saturn concern.

Matter precedes belonging—without mattering, there can be no belonging. Saturn can teach us the kind of dignity only found by being told we don't matter (by a parent, a lover, an employer, a community, a school, a country, a world) but knowing deep in our bones that, in fact, we do. The kind of dignity Saturn accords us is the one that is *earned*, from the inside out. This dignity is not the status or comfort that is conferred by popularity, good opinion, or the writers of the canons. This dignity is the status we claim for ourselves by clawing our way out of the vilification, persecution, and gaslighting done to us by so-called authorities. Saturn teaches us to delve deeper, survive, and thrive against the meanness of the world.

Practice Pause

An old teacher of mine had a saying: "Stamp your own passport." It was his way of encouraging us to give ourselves the approval and permission we were seeking from some outside authority. It's actually a fun practice to catch yourself handing power over to someone, pining for their approval, and instead stamping your own passport.

Ask yourself: Where would I go, if I gave myself permission? What would I bring into being if I knew it mattered?

HARD WON VICTORIES

A March 2021 *Washington Post* article describes the multiple prison reform victories in Los Angeles County accomplished by the Black Lives Matter movement over four years:

- A multibillion-dollar jail contract was canceled by the county board of supervisors in favor of developing housing and health alternatives under the "care first, jails last" model.
- Measure R launched and passed, providing oversight of the jails and community input into the jail plan.
- Measure J passed, allocating 10 percent of LA county's discretionary budget ($360 million to $900 million a year) to housing, mental health, and substance abuse treatment as preventative measures for imprisonment.
- District attorney George Gascón was elected, who immediately after taking office issued policy changes such as stopping charging children as adults, ending sentencing enhancements, and not seeking the death penalty.

Saturn's victories are hard won, but they sure are sweet when they come.

EVOLUTIONARY COMPETENCIES: PILLARS OF SATURN

Saturn gives structure, efficiency, and integrity to our lives, our bodies, our communities, our activities, and our artistic expressions. He distills. He cuts out the fluff. "As the crow flies" is how he rolls. According to Vedic Astrology, crows are representatives of Saturn.

Based on astrological interpretations of current transits, we are moving into a new paradigm here on Earth where Saturn will steer us collectively in the direction of egalitarian structures, wider and simpler distributions of resources, decentralized operations, "open source" frameworks, and justice for all. What does that mean for each of us individually? How do those ideals come about?

GETTING TO WHAT MATTERS

When we have internalized the negative projections of others, we do not see ourselves clearly. This means we operate at less than full capacity as social beings. It means we do not have all our personal energy available to us.

One of the key evolutionary movements of Saturn is to strip away all false self-images to expose the truth that's been there all along. Though this is ultimately liberating, the process can be painful while it is happening. We have a lot invested in those false self-images, after all. But there is something so clean and freeing about divesting ourselves of the illusions and realizing the immense value of what we actually are.

Getting to what matters starts with this process of peeling back the layers of outer personas taken on in compensation for, or protection of, our vulnerable core. Once we arrive at our vulnerable core, though, we have struck the vein of gold. It is here we can mine for the rest of our lives, bringing out authentic expressions of our love and service to the world.

ADMITTING WHEN WE'RE WRONG AND HOLDING OURSELVES ACCOUNTABLE

"Oops." We don't have to self-flagellate or otherwise go overboard, but an important competency of Saturn is the ability to catch ourselves and say, "Oops. I goofed. I'm sorry. How can I make it up to you?" How simple this is, and yet how hard.

SELF-RESTRAINT

The "Honorable Harvest" is a way of being on the Earth that Robin Wall Kimmerer offers in her book, *Braiding Sweetgrass*. She describes the way her elders taught her to harvest plants and hunt animals: with presence, conscious reciprocation, and respect. Though the teaching is threaded throughout the whole book, one passage in particular spells out a very Saturn-rich understanding, coming from the Anishinaabe peoples:

> *The guidelines for the Honorable Harvest are not written down or even consistently spoken of as a whole—they are reinforced in small acts of daily life. But if you were to list them, they might look something like this:*
> *Know the ways of the ones who take care of you, so that you may take care of them.*
> *Introduce yourself. Be accountable as the one who comes asking for life.*
> *Ask permission before taking. Abide by the answer.*
> *Never take the first. Never take the last.*
> *Take only what you need.*
> *Take only that which is given.*

Never take more than half. Leave some for others.
Harvest in a way that minimizes harm.
Use it respectfully. Never waste what you have taken.
Share.
Give thanks for what you have been given.
Give a gift, in reciprocity for what you have taken.
Sustain the ones who sustain you and the earth will last forever.

The self-restraint involved in the Honorable Harvest is something we Westerners seem to have a hard time with. Taking only what we need has become an ambiguous matter, as *want* has blurred into *need* in our first world. Nonetheless, abiding by the spirit of the Honorable Harvest is the basis of sustainability for the whole of life on Earth—and a competency of Saturn.

Writing Prompt

Describe a situation you have a hard time accepting.

By accepting this situation, I am afraid that _____.

Read your statement out loud, and then read the following out loud:

I do not have to approve of this situation. I do not have to love the harm or the one creating the harm. Accepting does not mean I collapse into ineffectiveness, nor does it mean I stop working to change the situation. Accepting the situation means I get my life energy back.

THE LONG GAME

Working toward racial justice, environmental sustainability, or food justice isn't something that happens in the course of one lifetime or even one generation. We have to be in it for the long haul, maybe even for the next seven generations. Different courses of action, different strategies, accompany the different stages of the work.

At early stages, the goal is simply to survive with the goal intact. At early middle stages, the goal must be to carry on a fight for the importance of the work—defining how the work matters to us all as a human population. At later middle stages, the goal becomes to mobilize resources and energy toward the work in order to build critical mass behind the changes needed. At final stages, one chops wood and carries water. In other words, we continue to do the necessary and mundane daily tasks of sustaining a life.

No matter what stage of a Saturn journey you're in, the mantra is always, to quote Dory in *Finding Nemo*: "Just keep swimming. . . Just keep swimming. . ."

SATURN IS SEXY

Though our first reaction to Saturn events in our lives tend to shut us down with fear or humiliation or unworthiness, over the long run they offer the possibility of strengthening us. And that strength is sexy.

To register that sexiness in the world around us, though, requires looking through mature eyes. To mature eyes, sexiness is not something you can buy the right accessories for. Sexiness is cultivated over time in the way you respond to the things life throws at you. Mature sexiness is earned. I learned this the hard way through that relationship that almost took the wind out of me completely. After that experience, I am not attracted to the same things or people or places anymore. As my emotional life matured, so did my vision.

Now that I understand and work within the limitations of traumatic brain injury, my life is beginning to stabilize. Hallelujah! Much as I think fondly on those innocent notions I used to have, pre-diagnosis, of being able to do anything I wanted to do, knowing the actual parameters my brain dictates for my life is a huge relief. Much like a rebellious toddler tests the boundaries in order to know where they stand, and then feels more secure inside the structure those boundaries provide, I feel more secure inside my new parameters. Exercising prudence is not as sexy in the old way of looking at life. That is okay. Excelling within the new specs my life has for me is far more desirable to me from my new vantage point.

As a collective, we are testing Mother Earth's boundaries right now, just like a cranky toddler. She has already given us many indications of her parameters for us. As we take Saturn's evolutionary path and stay within the bounds, our collective lives may not look as sexy from the old point of view, but as we grow up and see with mature vision, the well-being and existential security we will have gained by living within Earth's ecological capacity will be loaded with allure.

PART IV:

SHADOW PLANETS

———

Every light has its shadow
Every future, its past
Bless our passage, Rahu-Ketu,
Through the course you cast

In Western Astrology, Rahu is known as the North Node of the Moon, and Ketu is known as the Moon's South Node. Western Astrology generally sees the North Node of the Moon as representing the karmic future and the South Node as the karmic past.

In Vedic Astrology, Rahu is known as the head of the dragon (a head without a body), and Ketu is known as the dragon's tail (a body without a head). Vedic Astrology sees Rahu as an augmentation of human experience and Ketu as a dispersion or reabsorption of human experience, kind of like the spider weaving its web (Rahu) and retracting the web's silk back into its own body (Ketu).

What the two systems agree on are the facts: Rahu and Ketu are not actual celestial bodies, rather they are astrologically significant, mathematically derived points in the sky related to eclipses. Since eclipses cast shadows on the two luminaries, the Sun and Moon, Rahu and Ketu are known as shadow planets. Together these two shadow planets represent the full range of shadow that can befall the spectrum of light and, in turn, the human organism.

Rahu and Ketu help us understand how to work most effectively with our free will in this lifetime by studying the course charted for us before we were born.

8

RAHU:
THE ANTHROPOCENE

——

"The pressures we exert on the planet have become so great that scientists are considering whether the Earth has entered an entirely new geological epoch: the Anthropocene, or the age of humans. It means that we are the first people to live in an age defined by human choice, in which the dominant risk to our survival is ourselves."

—ACHIM STEINER, UNITED NATIONS
DEVELOPMENT PROGRAM ADMINISTRATOR

A BIRD'S EYE

Often, when I met my friend, Nala, and her dog, Coco, at the large pond for a sunset dog walk and birding adventure, the green heron would appear. This was during a period in my life when I had returned to working in a more traditional nine-to-five job after many years working on my own. My walks with Nala were a necessary balm as I struggled to balance what felt like competing needs for financial stability, creative expression, and work that had impact. I would specifically come to visit the heron as if he were a trusted elder whose counsel I sought.

Nala and I walked the pond's edge a few times over the course of an hour, and she would hand me binoculars and explain what I was seeing. Tall trees lined the creek behind the pond in a dense screen. There we had seen solo songbirds, redtail hawks, and even a peregrine falcon one New Year's Eve. Robin, finch, cedar waxwing, sparrows, crow, junco, flicker, spotted towhee, hummers, chickadee, starling... any of these could be present on any given day. The pond and its surrounding waterways brought in the occasional river otter and probably, given its name "Bear Creek," wandering black bear. This little watering hole was one of the last vestiges of the more-than-human world, but around it loomed the I-5 freeway and homes for two-leggeds in all directions.

The green heron with his thick neck reminded me of a stout, aged man in a suit, smoking a cigar and drinking a bourbon alone in an old-timey bar. He had the air of a content, rugged individualist who played his role in pond culture but traveled solo. Dignified, independent, resourceful, and clever, his watchful demeanor let me know I was being watched just as much as I was watching.

On one particular day, I was moaning on at Nala about needing to leave my job. While there was nothing ostensibly wrong with the job or the company or the people I worked with, I simply felt out of alignment there. Nala was a great listener and conversationalist, and we probably did three laps of the pond with me yapping away when Coco abruptly stopped and looked at the other side of the pond. The heron had lit on a tucked away part of the shore, a rare change of position. Nala handed me the binoculars.

He hovered on stick-thin legs by the shore. He must have seen a possible meal of fish. We stood there in silence for a while, and I felt like the heron was communicating something to me about the predicament I was in about work. "You can find your fish anywhere," he seemed to say. "Just be patient."

Shortly after I quit that job and started up my astrology practice full-time again, I stopped seeing the green heron, though he had been there consistently over a period of a couple years. His work with me was done.

Rahu gives us access to whatever we consider to be "Other" than us—other peoples, other dimensions, extra-sensory, beyond the waking life, the *meta* physical. Whether from contact with the natural world, a boost given by technology, a high given by the "spirits" in a bottle, or communication with non-human entities, the augmentation of our daily waking experience is a gift of Rahu.

THE ASTROLOGICAL RAHU

According to ancient yogic cosmology, at the root of our existence is "consciousness"—that awake, aware, alive principle at the basis of who we are. Rahu is that part of our experience in this incarnation that pulls us forward, making us thirsty for more. We can't easily scratch the existential itch around what Rahu touches in our charts. It is a lifelong, endless yearning for more experience. Rahu was definitely at play in the scene from Ridley Scott's classic, *Blade Runner*, where Roy the replicant demands of his "father" Tyrell, "I want more life. . ."

Rahu is what entices consciousness into incarnation.

One way to locate Rahu in our own lives is through tracking our desire.

In the Western astrological classic *Astrology for the Soul*, Jan Spiller presents the widely accepted view in Western Astrology that Rahu (called the North Node of the Moon in that system) represents the karmic future. This is not incompatible with the Vedic way of thinking. The Soul's impulse for experience, after all, pulls us forward into our karmic future. In the Vedic way of apprehending Rahu, however, he is more specifically understood as *the force of desire itself* that pulls us forward into every new moment of experience.

BIGGER, BETTER, FASTER, MORE!

Unsteady, erratic, and sometimes ethically questionable, Rahu augments whatever it touches with a bit of urgency, perhaps over-zealousness, or even downright compulsion, obsession, or addiction and, when really out of balance, fanaticism. In aspect to another natal planet, Rahu makes that planet's goals loom larger than life in comparison to the rest of our experience. Rahu conjunct Moon, for example, can bring us into intimate contact (Moon) with other-than-human entities (Rahu), affecting our entire life experience.

Never too concerned with maintaining the status quo or fitting in, Rahu pushes the envelope for us wherever we humans are getting too predictable. Rahu takes us beyond the ordinary, beyond the mainstream, beyond the status quo.

On a subtler level, Rahu is about *enhancing* any human experience. Rahu represents where in our life and how we work with Energy and the technologies we use to do so. For our purposes in this chapter, Energy can be defined as the animating principle of the universe (electricity is to appliances as Energy is to the universe).

In the first world, our engagement with Rahu is primarily on technological levels. The augmentation of our own thinking capacity is an Energy we have harnessed that we don't question. We have cultivated its power and use it every day—we call it the internet.

An imbalanced Rahu in a chart can challenge a person to have necessary, appropriate boundaries between influences coming from other-than-human realms, like the internet, and this waking life. A person who has Rahu conjunct a challenged Mercury, for instance, might find themselves receiving unwanted communications from the dead, or a social media post of theirs might unintentionally go viral, bringing in all sorts of unwanted communications. Viruses are Rahu-style organisms through and through, by the way.

More indigenous cultures often have sophisticated ways of engaging with Energy in forms beyond our human being-ness, such as plant Energy, animal Energy, or spirit Energy. Mainstream ways of thinking in our Western world largely relegate working with Energy to "woo-woo," new age, or weirdo status. That's a true loss for us. Cultural relegation of these hidden domains of life as invalid does not concern Rahu. Just because human ignorance or denial or misinformation or lack of awareness labels Rahu experiences a certain way doesn't stop them from happening. The spirit worlds continue to influence and help us (and harm us) anyway. By dispossessing ourselves of the skillsets needed to interact with these worlds, we have put ourselves in tricky territory. Our Western world has so few qualified guides now because of the disdain we have for the Energy we cannot see.

The strand of Energy that represents Rahu in our lives takes notice when a deity is blessing our life; when the dead are interfering; when the land is teaching something; when the ancestors' influences come to bear on a situation; or when a protective spirit has our backs. These are more animist ways of understanding Energy that allow us to point to things we in the first world no longer consciously relate to because our awareness of these forces has atrophied through disuse.

Rahu competencies continue develope nevertheless, despite our Western culture's tendency to condemn and devalue them. Psychic ability, the ability to speak with the dead or plants or animals, and channeling ability are all examples of Rahu-like sensitivities. Imagine if we actually trained children who showed promise and interest in these realms. Imagine the kind of ethics and standards we might develop for these activities and how we might elevate them into the realm of usefulness—think, less Eleven from the Netflix hit series *Stranger Things* and more counselor Deanna Troi from *Star Trek*. Imagine how we would allow those gifted in these ways to give their gifts.

Of all the paths, the Rahu path of evolution is one that requires the most emotional and spiritual maturity. Without a firm basis in maturity, lifelong training in control of the senses, healing of the emotional body, and grounding in emotional neutrality, a Rahu-influenced person can do a lot of psychic damage by not understanding what they are working with or by being "taken over" by influences or energies beyond their control.

The Anthropocene Age we currently find ourselves in could be said to have a Rahu problem. With our collective human desire for bigger, better, faster, more, we have created the world of ecological overshoot we live in today. How do we work with Rahu to bring ourselves back into balance?

EVOLVING IN ENERGY

The evolutionary path of Rahu involves a lot of trial and error. It helps to have a qualified guide. And even then, the terrain can be bewildering and sometimes deadly. Rahu can bring riches or ruin, successes or madness. Rahu is best left to proven adepts in their fields. Rahu's effects are potent and must be approached with great reverence, respect, and care. Just as with handling fire during summer, deep inside a dry forest, much containment, experiential know-how, and safety precautions are needed.

One extra tricky feature of Rahu is that whatever Rahu influences perpetually changes. Not sitting still, constantly on the prowl for more, Rahu in contact with any other natal planet drives that planet to perennially pursue the thing it would otherwise approach more measuredly.

Because Rahu is related to the force of desire itself, Rahu brings life, augmented experience, excitement, change, and enhancement, but Rahu-driven gains are often inconsistent. Rahu can imbue the parts of the chart it touches with a "fool's gold" quality, making things appear more alluring to us, though on closer inspection we realize those things to be empty of the promise they seemed to have.

Rahu conjunct the Sun in the fifth house, for instance, might make fame look really good until we get there and realize our audience is not really seeing *us*—they are seeing what they want to project onto us. That same placement of Rahu conjunct the Sun in the fifth could instead find inner gold by being a great dad to his children, though that choice may not be visible until the person gets beyond the fool's gold glimmer of Rahu. (Being a great dad is not categorically better than fame. For some, fame is the choice in most alignment with their design.)

The evolutionary path of Rahu, for most of us, has to do with questioning our insatiable thirst and allowing for spaciousness to develop around it—with Rahu conjunct Mars, the thirst for peak performance; with Rahu conjunct Venus, the thirst to be beautiful or desirable or attractive; with Rahu conjunct Mercury, the thirst to know what can't be known through normal means.

Reining in Rahu requires the balancing force of Ketu—detachment. Just as the momentum of a speeding car takes a while to die down even when the brakes are applied, Rahu's momentum in our lives requires consistent reining in and patience. We need to take our foot off the gas, keep our wits about us, and steer.

Rahu's path of evolution is a *tantric* one, in the sense that it asks us to know ourselves through all of life rather than by a process of discerning the unreal from the real. Rahu embraces everything as real. Where Ketu's path involves withdrawal, Rahu's path is deeply engaged in the world. The trick is to know that the outer world will not ever fully quench your desire. We stop chasing the unreal mirage of water perpetually on the horizon. By not indulging your phantom thirst, you will be able to surf your desire all the way into the shore of unassailable self-awareness.

Writing Prompt

One way to work with Rahu is to spend time actively feeling our unlimited potential for experience. In expanding our identity to include everything, we loosen the chokehold Rahu has on us. (If I **am** everything, I don't need to go anywhere to experience anything. I can stay right where I am because all of life is within **me**.) This might feel conceptual at first. Allow yourself to play with it, and over time it will become a lived experience. Let this writing prompt help you discover the truth that "I am one with everything":

At the top of a blank page, write, "This Too, This Too Am I." Set a timer for one minute. You will be writing a list of things—absolutely anything that comes to mind—the only qualification for what you write is that it must be a noun. (e.g., glass, table, tree, sparkling diamond, lazy Sunday afternoon, blizzard,

toxic femininity, bodacious taco, washed-up minstrel, long and winding river finding its way to the
ocean, part-time genius). Write each new thing on
a new line. Both short and long lines are fine.

When you are done writing the list, read the list out
loud to yourself, putting "I am a(n)" before each line.

After you have read your own list, you may want
to read Thich Nhat Hanh's poem, "Please Call Me
by My True Names." (This famous poem is easily
accessed online.)

PLANT MEDICINE

Veena Leela has spent the better part of the last four years
in the Amazonian rainforest, studying with an indigenous
family of shamans there. Her tutelage regularly consists of
spending months at a time in the forest alone, learning from a
particular plant, taking in its medicine, then being guided by
it. This kind of training has the energetic signature of Rahu.

Veena's early experiences with Ayahuasca in Peru helped
to open her capacity to communicate with the unseen
world. For years before traveling to Peru, when Veena visited her parents in Pennsylvania, the forest near her parents' home was a place she would visit to make offerings to
the tribes who once lived on that land. She was moved to
create ceremony for them, offering tobacco and smoke for
their healing and liberation. On one particular medicine
journey in Peru, she was in Peru physically, "though, in my
experience with the medicine, I was back in the forest in

Pennsylvania," she remembers. "Then, in my experience in those woods again through the portal of Ayahuasca, there was a native chief from those lands, standing in front of me in the woods, and *he* was blessing *me* with tobacco smoke, reciprocating my ceremony for him and his people or the lineages that were there."

This "thinning of the veil" is an evolutionary function of Rahu. To become aware of what exists just beyond the veil (just as real and relevant as this waking life) requires a certain kind of Rahu orientation. In Veena's particular experience, it was facilitated through a plant medicine journey, though throughout the history of humans the adepts of different cultures found ways to travel there—through breathwork, through vision questing, through fasting, through austerities, through chanting, through dance.

Beyond the fascination of piercing through into alternative realities, these forms of travel have waking world benefits in terms of psychological wellness. Well-guided and well-supported plant medicine journeying can open up dimensions of experience that enhance or augment our capacity for deep emotional healing in our waking lives.

While Time heals much of the emotional wounding that occurs to us, sometimes we find residues of past wounds in our present-day emotional bodies. Plant medicine can help us close the loop on the past and the present. Veena describes what this process looks like as her present-day self "tending to a previous version of myself at a time where I was struggling or disconnected or just really on a subconscious level seeking deep healing."

Here is an example of this process, in Veena's words: "When I was really deep in the New York City nightlife scene and drugs, sometime in my teens/early twenties, I was in just a great deal of danger on all levels," she remembers. Then during an Ayahuasca ceremony she found herself back there in NYC, "carrying a quantum of medicine with me that I have been cultivating through different traditional healing work and also with the plant medicines, deliberately in the jungle. So, I'll use my breath as the vehicle of sending this healing, sending the medicine to my previous self and feeling how that ripple is empowering my present self." The breath links those two states, those two times.

Veena's training in the jungle has helped her navigate these states of awareness with more facility, being able to use her familiarity with these plants in assisting others in their own healing journeys. Traveling between states of awareness, or traveling between timelines, requires Rahu's evolutionary blessing and a whole lot of spiritual maturity.

DESIGNING THE FLOW OF ENERGY WITH TECHNOLOGY
In her book, *The Nature of Economies,* Jane Jacobs looks at how Energy flows through the natural world in order to understand how economies work. (She doesn't name it "Energy"; that's my word for it.) The book is a fictional conversation between friends, which makes the ideas she presents far more real and less intimidating than an economics textbook. The principles she proposes point along a Rahu trajectory of understanding the flow of Energy through our world.

Some of the book's foundational principles:

- We humans are an integral part of the natural world, rather than simply its consumers or destroyers. What we take and what we give *is part of* the natural world.
- "Economic life is ruled by [natural world] processes and principles we didn't invent and can't transcend, whether we like that or not. . . the more we learn of these processes and the better we respect them, the better our economies will get along."
- Working along with natural principles of development, expansion, sustainability, and correction, people can create economies that are more reliable than the ones we have now and that are also more harmonious with the rest of nature.
- Money is a feedback-carrying medium, one that both reports and responds to the feedback of the system.

Since money is a medium for Energy, wrapping our heads around the way our economies currently operate is part of Rahu's evolutionary journey. Each of our individual responsibility is part of it as well. None of us are neutral players in our economy; we are all active participants in natural world cycles of giving and receiving. That is why it is imperative we understand how we direct our Energy.

I got to know Ferananda Ibarra as a social innovator with a powerful intellect and a global reach. She is full of life and full of Energy. Her presence at community gatherings brings dynamic electricity into the room. She is the cofounder of the Metacurrency Project, which is helping to build the means (the patterns, principles, and protocols on which platforms may be built) for a new kind of economy. She also serves as the director of the Commons Engine, an organization which assists with currency design.

As I was preparing to write this chapter on Rahu, I knew I would need to tackle a subject I didn't yet fully grok. Even though I was an economics major for two years as an undergrad before switching to music, and then to English, and even though I had worked on a documentary film all about money, I still didn't understand exactly how any of these principles about money and currency flows applied to me. So, I turned to Ferananda for help.

"Nature is not about a tree, and a bush, and the soil," Ferananda offered. "Nature is about the interdependency between the tree and the bush and the soil and the microbiome and the mycelium at their roots that then connect and give them more Energy." This was an "Aha!" moment for me. Fer had just dislodged a remnant from the old paradigm in my mind of seeing the tree as an object rather than as part of the same system that I am part of.

Once we had established that, she further explained how the natural world and economies are related. A natural ecosystem is an Energy conduit: "The more Energy is reused and repurposed and goes to benefit more agents in that ecosystem, the more vibrant that ecosystem is." And, importantly, *economies function as ecosystems in this same way.*

My next question for Ferananda was, "What are we doing wrong? Why do we have economies that are clearly unsustainable, using up the Earth's resources faster than the Earth can replenish?"

She answered that we need to manage Energy flows better in order to stop all the dead end uses of Energy. Think, for example, of the large quantities of plastic that end up in landfills.

She elaborated, "Just look at the tropical forest and how it uses one single ray of light in incredible ways. One single sunbeam goes through the plant that through photosynthesis transforms it into sugar that goes to the mycelia, and then there's the animal that comes and eats the plant and then goes and poops and then there's the bird that comes and picks up the seed from the ground and then there's that flower that benefits from the bird's pollination. . . all these interdependencies that stem from one single stream of Energy. So, how can humans do that? How could *we* be better with the flow of Energy?"

In order to answer the questions Ferananda poses, we need to look at how we might become more conscious players in the flows of Energy we are already engaged in.

Ferananda and her Metacurrency cofounder, Arthur Brock, propose that part of the difficulty with more conscious participation is how opaque these Energy flows are to us still. First, we need to be able to *see* and *identify* these inherent Energy flows within all the living systems in which we take part. For example, what if anytime we bought something, the flow of our consumption was made visible to us? What if when you bought an item from the store you had a visual, not just of the numerical price, but of the actual Energy flows attached to purchasing that item—from the original materials for the product being sourced; to all the hands and efforts that went into creating that product; to all the paths traveled for that product to be assembled; to the waste created in the making of that product; to how well that company treated its employees as the product arrived on the shelf?

In this hypothetical visual, you would also see the money you pay for the product, and how that money goes to the company who made it and what they do with that money. Once we start *seeing* these flows and connecting the dots, then we can make more conscious, more sustainable choices. Our decisions then shape the market by giving it the right signals: No, I will not buy a product whose flows are jammed up with dead end choices like poisoning the environment, because that cuts off a needed flow of Energy from the environment. When we don't see these flows, we are more likely to resort to unconscious consumerism and its busted flows.

CURRENCY DESIGN

Referring back to the Venus chapter where I spoke about the concept of the commons, how will we design currencies that capture a more vibrant, dynamic interplay between humans and our commons? If we start with the premise that all of the natural world is a commons, what kind of a dance do we want to dance with that commons? The current economy dance has us tripping and falling down a lot. Is that the extent of our imagination? How can we design systems that will allow us all to thrive; that will allow us to live in harmony with the natural world we are part of?

This is where Ferananda's work comes in. "The design of our social agreements, our governance, our economies, and even our architecture will create specific social outcomes. So, we need to be mindful in how we design social systems that don't recreate the extractive patterns we currently have." A centralized system, for instance (useful in some scenarios), gives authority to one entity, whereas a decentralized system designs for shared authority between its members, acknowledging and bringing in the intelligence from everywhere in the group, even at the edges.

Might decentralized systems be more equitable choices for social media platforms? For example, Facebook is centralized. Our data is owned by Facebook; we, the end users, have no decision-making capacity; decisions come from the top down and affect us in ways we are not aware of. A decentralized social media platform would be agent-centric, meaning agents are the focus rather than the data; the platform is governed by its users. Such a platform would theoretically be able to design for diversity, wellbeing, and healthy flows of communication and coordination a central entity is not able to capture. Decentralized systems tend to have more resilience. (Healthy ecosystems are not monocrops, where a single point of failure can bring the entire system down.)

Holochain, one of the projects Ferananda has collaborated on, is an open-source framework for building peer-to-peer applications. Let that sink in for a minute. It means that no central entity owns the tools to the framework, and no central entity owns every user's data. Each agent owns their own data. Holochain attempts to solve for more equitable social outcomes in harmony with the natural world. It does this through a unique "distributed ledger technology" (a kind of "post Blockchain" technology that aims for "digital agency," putting power back into the hands of the people using the technology.) Holochain is one of many distributed, decentralized, open-source technologies coming on the scene offering us alternative ways to better design our Energy flows. Rahu would be impressed.

After my conversation with Ferananda, I felt like my operating system had just gotten a long overdue upgrade. I was excited to start applying this new-felt sense of my own participation in the flows of our economy in my own life.

Practice Pause

Take a minute to visualize your participation in the Energy flows of your life.

Close your eyes and see all the resources coming in—your income stream, a meal someone cooks for you, the relaxation you derive from a particular environment, hugs, the dreamtime, and every single thing that you buy—anything that represents Energy coming "in."

Then also see how you send that Energy out—paying people for their services, tending a garden, cooking and sharing a meal with someone, maintaining a home space so the others in your home are supported, feeding an animal, giving a hug, doing your sacred work.

Spend a few moments visualizing the actual Energy itself, as it flows through your life. What shape does it take? What is its geometry, speed, movement style?

EVOLUTIONARY COMPETENCIES: CHANNELING RAHU

Rahu evolutionary competencies require understanding the very nature of desire. Understand, first and foremost, that desire will never be fully satisfied. That is its nature. Once we comprehend that, next is *not chasing* the desire that we know will never end. When the pursuit ends, the heat of the desire dies down a bit.

In my experience, it does not work to deny that the desire is present. This will just make it burst the seams and come out sideways. It is better to be intimately aware of the desire and acknowledge its presence, while seeking moderation in its fulfillment.

Once this shadowboxing with desire is understood, then the next step of Rahu's evolution becomes possible: working skillfully with Energy.

DESIRE AIKIDO

We might look more deeply into the nature of desire. Isn't it interesting how opposites attract? Why is it that magnetism draws two poles together, always toward unification?

Wherever infatuation arises in you, you are coming face to face with a magnetic pull inside your own psyche toward an opposite pole, something possibly not expressed in you. Whenever you notice the quality of being carried away by an attraction, maybe being thrown off your own center a little bit, infatuation is probably at play. Time spent "having" or "possessing" that opposite pole—whether in the form of wealth, a lover, success, freedom, excellence—tends to integrate some of that pole within us, bringing the wide swing of the poles a bit closer together.

What if we could work with desire in a way that lessened the problematic obsession to possess? What if it were possible to be in a kind of *Aikido* with desire, working with its flow but not getting swept away by it, allowing its movements but never going unconscious in the having of a thing? Working in this way with desire can help us slow down and surf the urgency that often comes with Rahu.

One viable way to surf that urgency is to actively practice letting go. When your inner urge to have that object of desire is seemingly uncontrollable, get quiet and sit with the discomfort. Go deeper. Ask yourself what will happen if you don't "get" that object of desire. Let yourself go there and feel those feels. Take some time and *give yourself* whatever it is you think the person or place or situation will give you.

RELATING VERSUS OTHERING

Rahu traditionally represents foreigners; "them"; the Other. Particularly relevant right now in the early part of the twenty-first century is an examination of who and what we consider to be "Other," especially since all of us on Earth are ultimately part of one organism.

Animist values and practices might come in handy for such an examination. On his website, animist author and educator Dr.

Daniel Foor draws a parallel between social toxins of misogyny and white supremacy as hinging upon "seeing other-than-male and other-than-white people as less than full persons, less worthy of respect." In order to sustain such supremacy-based perceptions, we have to think of "those" people as "other" than us. If we happen to fear what we don't understand, what is foreign to us, what is "other" than us, we won't take care of those "others" like we would those who belong to "us."

Dr. Foor encourages us to instead see the natural world as extended family: "Many humans tend to devalue and objectify our other-than-human kin in similar ways. The global ecological crisis sources largely from the tendency, especially among modern industrialized nations, to see the rest of the natural world only in terms of human desires. When we see things rather than people, resources rather than relatives, we are no longer accountable to the rest of life. Conversely, when we view animals, plants, and others as extended family, we are more likely to relate with them in ethical ways."

Rather than othering, if we can bring ourselves into conscious relationality with all those humans and other-than-humans we currently think of as "other," we will be walking Rahu's evolutionary path.

RECIPROCITY

Rahu imbalances mostly stem from the lack of understanding that any Energy we might relate with relates back to us. And vice versa.

If I receive a piece of fruit from a tree, I am in relationship with that tree, the sunlight that fed it, the rain that watered it, the soil and mycelia that support it in *its* web of relations. I have become a part of that web of relations by receiving the tree's fruit. I take into my own body that tree's web of relations when I eat the fruit. What Energy will I give back to the tree? At the very least I can reciprocate with the Energy of gratitude. Maybe I will even trim a dead branch for the tree or help bring the tree water in a dry season.

Developing and deepening our sense of all the ways we participate in flows of reciprocity, cyclic Energy flows helps us come into right relationship with Rahu, the force of engagement and intimacy with life that propels us ever onward.

WAIT FOR THE OPENING

The other day I saw a green heron flying down a creek, wings outstretched wide. The ridiculously wide wingspan of a heron is always a headscratcher for a bird its size. They truly sail the air just above the water and are a thrill to behold in flight.

Heron stopped on a dirt and rock outcropping, and I got to spend some time with him again, from the other side of the creek. I could feel that he was aware I was there and was tolerating my presence. I promised him I would stay really still and not foil his chances of supper. It was a thrill to be in his presence once again. It was as if I had sidled up to him at the bar with his bourbon in hand, and we were about to enjoy a private joke together.

We both stayed there, quite still, for a long time. People came and went, the creek flowed between us, and time took on a different rhythm. I finally felt the space between us settle and felt myself drop down into my body, observing how keenly he took in his environment. I noticed my vision shift, more attuned to the way light was moving on the creek. What was he seeing, or hearing, or feeling, I wondered. What was it like to be him?

When I sensed an opening between us, I silently thanked him for the teaching he had given me all those years ago. He looked at me, looked at the water, and with a movement so fast my eye did not register it, he snapped at the water and pulled out a tiny fish. He shot me a glance, long enough for me to see the fish in his mouth, threw it back in his gullet, and was off, air-hover-sailing the creek again.

Moments like these are precious beyond words to me. In coming into relationship with this winged-one over the years, my connection with all of life has been strengthened. This kind of connection is at the better end of Rahu's gifts.

9

KETU: ETERNITY AS THE END OF TIME

"Man discovers that he is nothing else than evolution become conscious of itself."

—JULIAN HUXLEY

"The universe continues to evolve. And yes, every one of our body's atoms is traceable to the big bang and to the thermonuclear furnaces within high-mass stars that exploded more than five billion years ago. We are stardust brought to life, then empowered by the universe to figure itself out—and we have only just begun."

—NEIL DEGRASSE TYSON

A TEMPLE IN SOUTH INDIA

Peacocks crow outside the open-air temple. The thick, sweet perfume of India dances around the meditators sitting on the floor every time a minor breeze rustles one of the city block wide trees outside. Everything about this place feels impossible and primordial.

I've kicked off my chappals in a hurry, in the sandals pile by the entrance. My feet embrace the cool of the glazed concrete floor. Not much fanfare adorns this temple. Unlike most Hindu temples in India, this one is more of a meditation hall than place for Brahmin priest ritual. I have come to southeastern India shortly before the rainy season, the coolest season in Tiruvanamalai, like most Westerners do, and the heat still presses mercilessly. The bustle and hum of India spools just outside the temple, but inside a profound stillness permeates the space, making it easy to close your eyes and come out of meditation an hour later.

Most pilgrims here are in their fifties and sixties. I am in my early thirties and have come to stay at Ramana Maharshi's ashram. Ramana is a spiritual teacher whose mode of self-inquiry hit me like a ton of bricks back in Los Angeles. Who knew his simple mantra, "Who am I?" explored in meditation, could strike gold?

Meditation today begins like any other day but takes a different course than usual. I follow the breath. I use the mantra. This doesn't turn off the discursive mind but does put it on the periphery, in a similar fashion to how I tune out the crowing peacocks. I sink deeper and deeper into a space that I distinctly recognize as more familiar, more me, more always here, unchanging, than anything else. Deep meditation will take over quickly, I realize, so "take note of this entrance gate quickly!" the mind flashes as the distinctions between things start to blur.

There in the blue black stillness, that eternity with no other source than itself reveals itself. First like a grand vista being apprehended in all its vastness. Then more like a warm bath. Then more like the feeling of home. There is rest there. And stillness. And nothing at all. And everything.

There, I am eternity, looking at itself.

Who knows how long in earthly time later, the first thought, coming from a panicked body, arises: "Could I stay here forever?"

When "I" begin to come back, so too do the layers, the perimeters of being. First, the sense of me returns—the habitual concern for my well-being, always a quiet anxiety beneath the surface of everything, the patterned sense of being inside a body. Then thoughts, almost like yesterday's leftovers in the fridge, "How long was I in meditation?" and "I wonder what peacocks eat. . ." Finally, sensations return—I am aware of sweat beads necklacing down my back, the sounds of people and peacocks and monkeys, and the cacophony of smells. How long was I gone? I don't know, but as I open my eyes the light has shifted, and with it the weight of the day.

Just before me, a small peacock feather sits on the ground by my knee. Glorious and perfect, I take it home to the US with me, where it will always stay on a home altar, reminding me of a day in a temple in India, where I discovered who I was not.

Our discovery of who we really are is often accompanied by precise learnings of who we are not. These often come as a kind of Ketu-induced attrition of the "separate self"—the one who thinks they are separate from all of life, with a separate identity, who is in it for him or herself. This one gets to recede into the background little by little, as the full magnificence of one's true identity is revealed, becomes foreground, and serves as our base of operations in this human life.

THE ASTROLOGICAL KETU

Where Rahu is the force of desire, Ketu (pronounced Kay-too) is the inward pull of detachment. What goes up, must come down.

Ketu is the water we swim in. Who we present as in this life, from Ketu's perspective, is a myth, a mirage, a flimsy construction held together with only the most anemic of justifications, excuses, and compelling stories. But this is because Ketu knows we are so much more than what we think we are.

The popular awareness, "We are Spirit having a human experience," is Ketu 101. Ketu's whole agenda is to get us to develop enough detachment that we might become still enough inside our lives to notice who and what we truly are at the end of the day when all is said and done.

"What, of who I am, is eternal?"

Ketu is what withdraws consciousness back into itself; back into Source.

It is Ketu that gets us to recall the web we've spun into the world. It's that nagging feeling we get when we've accomplished all we've set out to do and realize we've been chasing our tail; that there's something more real, deeper, more intimate, more significantly true that we long to dissolve into.

But with Ketu, the holy grail we seek is not to be found outside ourselves in the tangible world. What we seek can only be found in the landscapes where Spirit resides. Ketu doesn't care which religion, or cosmology, or set of cultural practices a human enters the land of Spirit from. Not of this world, Ketu invites us all into the Spirit-based mystery of who we are.

Ketu's influence is not usually very fun. In fact, by definition, Ketu takes the fun out of a thing, if not only for us to lean more in the direction of Rahu, where our desire is meant to help us develop our Soul's integrity while in a human suit.

Ketu can be a real problem-causer for worldly life. Transits of this non-entity or Spirit can set off cataclysms in our material world, change things beyond recognition, obfuscate or even make invisible, and sneakily destroy our best-laid plans. The thing is, Ketu doesn't do this to be a jerk. It does it when source energy is ready to return home to itself. For instance, we might accomplish something spectacular and receive no recognition or reward for it. The feeling of emptiness this may trigger can be a doorway into the goal of all spiritual practice.

People with a prominent Ketu in their chart often have less interest in the world than those around them. They are in a constant practice of letting go, of detaching. Yet they can present with a kind of intensity and fervor that makes them seem willful. Terrorism is a Ketu-ruled activity, for instance. But Ketu acting through someone who has shed many layers of identification with false selves is a thing to behold, an uplifting force to be around. The Dalai Lama, for instance, has his natal Sun not far from Ketu.

Ketu is not entirely a wet blanket. Ketu's position in our charts shows us what gifts we bring with us from the past. These might be the parts of our lives that our ancestors have fully developed and passed down to us through our gene pool, like artistic ability or a way with people, or an interest in applied kindness. Ketu's gifts are readily available to us in this lifetime. We don't have to work for them. They're just there.

EVOLVING IN SPIRIT

An Agent of Evolution will want to work rigorously with the idea of detachment. When we suffer it is easy to confuse compensations we make (like dissociation) for detachment. Being able to discern the difference between the two is vital.

When a person is running a *spiritual bypass* on something unpleasant, for instance, there is the unmistakable energy signature of aloofness that would quickly change to anxiety if the person had to navigate the other person or situation they were avoiding. Detachment, on the other hand, is an energy signature that broadcasts, "I have nothing to latch onto, nothing to fight, no agenda," even while in the process of engaging with the most Machiavellian unpleasantry.

As humans, this is not easy for us. Built into our bodies are survival instincts and needs for human touch and companionship, for being seen, and for giving our gifts. Ketu doesn't ask us to ignore these very real human dimensions.

It simply asks us to keep our awareness rooted in Spirit that is the true source of our identity, which means we cannot allow ourselves to get wrapped up in or overly identified with something we know will pass with time. . . As all things do.

Writing Prompt

Connecting with Ketu's aliases in your life can be a breadcrumb trail leading you to Ketu's deeper gifts.

Write a list of the blessings and burdens you have received from your ancestors—all the resources, personality traits, interests, fears, orientations, and anything else you think of that are their legacy to you. At the end of this list, thank your ancestors, somewhat like this: "Praise and blessings to my Ancestors. Thank you for the gift of life. Teach me how to embody your blessings for all my relations. May you be at peace."

(This writing prompt is inspired by a prayer recited during an ancestral medicine training by Dr. Daniel Foor. Check the resources section for more information on ancestor reverence ritual.)

INVOLUTION AS EVOLUTION

There is a Yin and a Yang to evolution—an inbreath and an outbreath. Some parts of evolution are active, requiring that we learn something, practice something, and grow. Other aspects of evolution require us to cede our dreams, plans, identities, histories, and control.

ENDINGS

Endings are Ketu's domain. That feeling of dissatisfaction that causes shrinkage, absence, or detachment—that is often the beginning of an ending—is Ketu at work. In the same way that arriving at most deeply rooted spiritual gains requires some self-sacrifice, some letting go, some austerity, and some ending, Ketu represents areas of our lives that get shrouded in mists and circled in invisibility, or riddled with so much change and strange lack of direction as to loosen our grasp in those areas.

Buddhist teachings on detachment are helpful in areas of life where Ketu is at play. Detachment doesn't mean we can't have the thing. It just means we practice not clinging, not clutching, not grasping even as we enjoy what we have. One teacher of mine would make a gesture to demonstrate this quality of detachment—he would suspend his open hand in the air, palm side up. I would often imagine a hummingbird sitting there in his palm, so delightful... Always free to stay, or to go.

We don't hold on. We know that all things begin and end. We know that Love itself never leaves. We get better at the endings.

SHADOW WORK

Psychological shadow work—meeting the darker parts of our psychological selves—is also Ketu's domain. Just as Ketu shows us what blessings we have brought into this life with us (whether our own from past lives, the blessings of our lineages that lie in our DNA, or the resources we are born into), Ketu also shows us the lineage burdens, precise locations of absence, and darkness we bring in with us.

At the root of most spiritual development is the necessity to face things we would rather not face—things like a feeling of not being good enough, or a habit of thinking we are entitled to whatever we want, or a jealous streak. None of our own personal demons are fun to face, but when we do, we free up life energy. That vital force inherent in all of us gets diverted to shadow expression when we are not aware of our shadow.

HEALING TRAUMA

Often, psychological shadow work brings up the necessity to work on bringing Presence to the parts of ourselves that have been traumatized and are stuck in earlier stages of development. Working with trauma falls under Ketu's realm. Those parts of our experience that are stuck in painful, patterned responses show us where we might want to shine Ketu's flashlight to see what's (not) there.

A mentor of mine used to illustrate the interdependence of the individual, the collective, and consciousness itself with a metaphor about the drop, the wave, and the ocean. We instantly get that the drop is not separate from the wave or the ocean. Similarly, the individual (the drop) is not separate from the family system or any other collective system it participates in (the wave); nor is the individual separate from Consciousness itself (the ocean). The drop, wave, and ocean are simply different kinds of "wrappers" that conscious awareness can come in.

In individual therapeutic situations, often what we are attending to in the drop is actually a condition of the wave. Without understanding the way that trauma has its roots in our family systems and collectives, we put an enormous amount of pressure on the individual to solve or heal things that cannot be solved or healed beyond behavioral modifications without going deeper into the roots of collective trauma.

PRESENCE AND ABSENCE

I met Laura Calderon de la Barca in a global online class of Thomas Hübl's. She facilitated a BIPOC (Black, Indigenous, people of color) breakout group looking specifically at racial trauma. I instantly felt a kind of *simpatico* with Laura, possibly because of the multi-racial heritage we both carried, she a Mexican mestiza, half Indigenous, half Spanish, and I a first-generation American, half German, half South Asian. When Laura spoke, I felt new dimensions open up in my body that normally remained closed, as if more of me could be present. She was embodying both her indigenous and Spanish roots simultaneously, without collapsing into binaries.

Laura is a psychotherapist and scholar addressing individual and collective trauma in Mexico. She hosts and co-hosts large programs aimed at collectives—collectives as small as a family and as large as her home country of Mexico. One of her projects aims to provide services toward "a healthy, creative Mexico, capable of assuming its role in the world."

Her passion for collective healing began organically when the pain of her own experience led her to pursue individual healing. She shares how she inherited a sense of defeat which, through a deep and powerful healing process, revealed to her its *collective* nature. It started out as a painful, horrible experience anytime she would speak in public to a group. Though she was academically accomplished and confident about the topics she would speak on, whenever she stood in front of a group of people, she would feel contracted, wanting to hide. The experience was puzzling, because she had already done so much deep personal work in therapy by that time.

Finally, a mentor helped her find that missing puzzle piece in her own healing. Both of Laura's parents were raised by single mothers, and growing up in Catholic Mexico, this brought shame. Her mentor's insight into the collective and intergenerational nature of the trauma helped her to see the connection between the horrible feelings of wanting to hide when speaking in front of groups and the shame of her parents. She recognized that the shame was not her own—that she had, in effect, "inherited" it. She went to the depths of her shame, the depths of her rage, the depths of her terror, to undo this artifact of inherited trauma, but every time she resurfaced from those depths she felt revitalized, having recovered more and more of her true self. Back to the drop, wave, ocean metaphor, Laura as the drop needed to understand the nature of the wave she was part of in order to return to her true nature as the ocean.

Once she was able to recognize the mechanism of collective trauma in herself, she began seeing it everywhere, realizing the social epidemic it currently proves to be. She thought to herself, "What would the world be like if everybody who's hurting from [collective trauma] would be freed? The world would be a completely different place!" This vision of what is possible for our world motivated Laura to devote her life to bringing this insight to as many people as possible.

Laura's individual work eventually led to training in group work on healing collective trauma with Thomas Hübl. She describes a key discovery from those trainings:

> *Thomas would say to us, "Feel the space between us."*
> *[Through this instruction] I became aware of the space*
> *between us as alive, as responsive, as full of information,*
> *that had its own flow, that we are also part of.*

Laura describes a memory of her first true experience of feeling "the space between us": "I was in a course. . . All of a sudden, I started to feel as though I was immersed in some gel that every single person in the room was also immersed in, and every movement everyone made I could feel. Every person raising their eyebrow, every movement of an arm, every turning of a head. . . I could feel the whole thing, from everybody, in one moment. I was blown away." This vivid experience of Laura's gave her a somatic experience she could recognize as matching what Thomas Hübl described as "the space between us."

When many of a group's participants become conscious of that space between them, the space has been potentiated for healing collective trauma. Thomas Hübl and others call this active participation in a group's shared space collective "coherence," which can be practiced and cultivated. Some of us are motivated by the possibility of reducing suffering in others. Some of us feel more fully alive in that field. Whatever our motivation for exploring collective coherence in holding a space for the healing of collective trauma, through spiritual practice and training with other adepts, we can all learn to do this.

Space and Spirit are connected. When the space between us is full of alive presence, you have Spirit, or consciousness. When the space between us holds vacuums, or absence, you have trauma. In the work of Thomas Hübl and his organization, collective coherence is introduced to places where the space between us has been shattered. They bring Presence to absence.

Healing collective trauma is work done in community. Ketu's evolutionary road leads in this direction.

Practice Pause

Many composers and musicians, from Miles Davis to Claude Debussy, recognize how the music comes alive when you "play the space between the notes." What if we do a similar exercise for life? What would it be like to "be the space between all the things of the world"? Set a timer for two minutes, close your eyes, and see what it is like to be the space that holds all the things of this world, including your own body.

THE RELATIONSHIP BETWEEN
WAKING UP AND HEALING TRAUMA

"Recent studies and discoveries increasingly point out that we heal primarily in and through the body, not just through the rational brain. We can all create more room and more opportunities for growth in our nervous systems. But we do this primarily through what our bodies experience and do—not through what we think or realize or cognitively figure out."

—RESMAA MENAKEM

The mythological underpinnings of Vedic Astrology symbolize Ketu as a body without a head; whereas Rahu is symbolized as a head without a body. Metaphysically, one interpretation of this symbolism is that Ketu represents our somatic experience—the experience stored in the cells of our body.

The field of trauma studies is burgeoning with examples of the importance of addressing trauma *in the body.* One of the field's progenitors, psychiatrist Bessel Van der Kolk, wrote about working with trauma in the body in scholarly articles in the 1990s and more recently in his book, *The Body Keeps the Score.* Not only is trauma stored in the body's somatic memory, the release of trauma also happens through our bodies.

Increasingly, the field of epigenetics is finding that our ancestors' traumatic experiences are heritable. An article printed in the *New York Times* in 2018 explains:

> *The idea is that trauma can leave a chemical mark on a person's genes, which then is passed down to subsequent generations. The mark doesn't directly damage the gene;*

there's no mutation. Instead, it alters the mechanism by which the gene is converted into functioning proteins, or expressed. The alteration isn't genetic. It's epigenetic.

For the past decade, the field of epigenetics has been generating studies on everything, from the descendants of Holocaust survivors, to victims of poverty, to those who experienced famine, examining the heritability of trauma. The same *New York Times* article suggests this takeaway:

> *If these studies hold up, they would suggest that we inherit some trace of our parents' and even grandparents' experience, particularly their suffering, which in turn modifies our own day-to-day health—and perhaps our children's too.*

Somatic abolitionist and racial trauma healing expert Resmaa Menakem explains how racial trauma compounds itself: "The answer to why so many of us have difficulties is because our ancestors spent centuries here under unrelentingly brutal conditions. Generation after generation, our bodies stored trauma and intense survival energy and passed these on to our children and grandchildren." We know that trauma is stored in somatic memory. (Van der Kolk, 1994) Are diseases like diabetes and heart disease possibly our inherited *responses to* trauma?

Not only do we have our own, individual, biological trauma to contend with, but as social beings, we also participate in fields of collective trauma. Laura Calderon de la Barca defines collective trauma as "a catastrophic event or process that disarticulates the fundamental fabric and the basic structures that our society has created to sustain its way of life." Living with collective trauma is an invisible reality; to make an analogy that seeks to make it more visible, it would be sort of like trying to live in a house where staircases are missing, the plumbing is in disrepair, and mice have overrun the closets and pantries.

One recent high-profile event that fits the bill of collective trauma is the coronavirus pandemic of 2020. Worldwide systems have been permanently altered, and our trust of social engagement has been rocked and polarized. Its impact will likely remain in the collective human psyche until the trauma finds healing and resolution. None of us know how, when, or if that will happen, but I believe it is possible.

As Laura explains, collective events like pandemics and natural disasters don't have nearly the same traumatic impact that collective events like racism, colonialism, or genocide do. With these kinds of human-on-human inflicted violence, the very foundations of our social fabric and interdependencies that usually support our healing are destroyed. The fracture of our social foundations buries these traumas even deeper and makes them more difficult to address. Yet address them, we must.

Trauma's impacts on humans is biological, as the field of epigenetics is also finding. Perhaps in some future time the Surgeon General of the United States will name racial trauma from colonization of the Americas and racial trauma from slavery the public health epidemics they are.

So much of our human potential currently lies tied up in trauma. Our potential in this life to enjoy good health, good relationships, fulfilling work, fulfilling social lives, connection with the natural world—all of these are at risk when trauma is not addressed.

From the Soul's point of view an even more tragic reality lies underneath the individual not being able to express its full potential during a lifetime. The "awakening" or "self-realization" possible for the individual is not sustainable in the presence of trauma, as trauma is a set of automatic biological responses that hijack a body's freedom. Although awake awareness is always present, witnessing everything the body will experience, endure, and relish, the presence of trauma puts the body in a feedback loop of painful, individual, stuck identity. Instead of "Moksha," or spiritual liberation, trauma by definition binds.

This is why the work of healing trauma is critical. The work is lifelong and arduous. There are no real worldly rewards to doing this work. It is the work of the bodhisattvas—beings who dedicate themselves to liberating all sentient life from suffering—among us.

EVOLUTIONARY COMPETENCIES: KETU'S HOUSE OF MIRRORS

The primary evolutionary movement of Ketu is to reveal to us the emptiness at the core of all experience. This can be an existentially painful thing to discover. So, Ketu's particular path of evolution could be considered the final doors we pass through in spiritual life.

Very few people willingly volunteer for the existential crisis Ketu brings. Most of us arrive there because the pain of life makes us search for something deeper, more meaningful, more eternal. Laura Calderon de la Barca admits she sought out healing because the experience of collective trauma "was so painful for me, it was so disabling. I was so scared that my life would go by and it would have not been the life I was born for."

Seeking out Ketu's path of evolution is not necessary. To do so would not be coming from a life-affirming place, and furthermore, anything in you that would seek it out, would seek it out for the wrong reasons. It will come to find you when the time is right.

If Ketu's path of evolution is knocking on your door, then this chapter is written for you.

GETTING BETTER AT ENDINGS

How well we end something is more important to our Soul's development than how we begin. Beginning is easy and often fun. Ending is often difficult and painful. But how we end anything—a marriage, a job, a stint in a city, our youth, affiliation with a particular community, our life... these endings determine how much baggage we take into the new beginnings. Since Ketu's ultimate goal is spiritual liberation, which means freedom from all identities, all karma, all trauma, all ties that bind, the more we can free ourselves as we end a thing, the better.

Getting better at endings requires staying present, feeling all the feels, releasing all the feels, not latching on to any part of the pain with any new identity like "I always fail at marriage," or "I will never be able to do work I love." Instead, know that everything changes and, eventually, everything ends.

FACING OUR SHADOW

"Whether individual or collective, our shadows cannot simply be buried and forgotten; they will haunt us until we return them to life. And if we never do, they will haunt our children and our children's children, passing each to the next in an endless repetition of karma and time."

—THOMAS HÜBL

Facing our shadow requires emotional literacy. It took me until age fifty before I could properly identify when I was feeling fear. Due to complex trauma, fear didn't register on my inner radar. It took decades of therapy and ultimately it took exploring trauma somatically, noticing the signs my body was giving me, to understand that absent, vacuous feeling was actually a feeling of fear. Since the feeling was unconscious to me, it was, by definition, part of my "shadow."

I trained for a time with a gifted psychotherapist named Robert Augustus Masters. With Robert, in intensive group scenarios, we studied the emotions live, in ourselves, in others, in groups. Working with shadow, in ourselves and in others, was an art form, and we were all artists in training. Shadow arises for each of us on the daily. We have plenty of material to work with, right where we are.

Because shadow is by definition not visible to ourselves, it is critical to have a qualified facilitator to help guide you across that terrain. Most therapists can serve that role. Some astrologers also have those skills.

HEALING INDIVIDUAL, COLLECTIVE, AND INTERGENERATIONAL TRAUMA

"Resilience is built into the cells of our bodies. Like trauma, resilience can ripple outward, changing the lives of people, families, neighborhoods, and communities in positive ways. Also like trauma, resilience can be passed down from generation to generation."

—RESMAA MENAKEM

In the enlightenment and awakening the Eastern wisdom traditions such as Buddhism and Hinduism point to, a person's conscious awareness has been freed from the trance of identifying with all the small concerns of a limited, individual self.

With the fissures of trauma running through the nervous system, the spiritual awakening that Ketu is known for granting will not sustain itself. The body will pull the local consciousness back into the trance of the individual self, or back into "sleep."

So, working on healing individual trauma is essential for Ketu's path of evolution. Because we can inherit our ancestors' trauma, healing intergenerational trauma is essential for Ketu's path of evolution. And because we are ultimately not separate, because we are all in this together, healing our collective trauma is essential for Ketu's path of evolution.

Doing this work begins with being witnessed. Healing happens in the company of people who have done their own work and have developed the resilience to stay compassionately, non-judgmentally present in the face of absence. While much healing can happen in solitude, the full healing of trauma is not done solo—it is done in the context of skilled relationality. In his book, *Healing Collective Trauma*, Thomas Hübl explains, "Mutual presence and group witness are the foundations of collective trauma work."

OUR GREATEST GIFT: OUR PRESENCE

Thomas Hübl offers his own wisdom and the wisdom of many experts on the healing of trauma when he states:

> *Trauma work can be a kind of spiritual search-and-rescue mission. It does not require that we endlessly revisit every tortured experience, crying, shouting, or talking it through. But we must locate our disembodied ghosts, buried somewhere in that frozen grave of the dissociated self. Our work is to liberate our [fragmented selves] with the reclaiming energies of integration and love. To revive and restore them back into the body, through the central channel, reintegrating all of our parts into the whole of our essence."*

Part of Thomas Hübl's mission is to "contribute to the healing of collective and intergenerational trauma, and to reduce its disruptive effects on our global culture." It takes a large group that has been steeping in this work for some time to be effective in witnessing and bringing presence to collective trauma. Hübl's organization hosts intensive trainings for people around the world to do this vital, sacred work.

Whether you find yourself called to the greater group effort, or whether you address your own trauma, you engage in an act of love and integration on behalf of the collective.

MAGIC RUBY SLIPPERS

Becoming enlightened while meditating in a cave is one thing. Staying enlightened down off the mountain, smack in the middle of the marketplace, is another thing entirely. Or better yet, while sitting with family at Thanksgiving dinner.

My time in India at Ramana's ashram allowed me to peek behind the curtain, revealing my own private Wizard of Oz pulling his levers, booming my own constructed reality in a familiar but farcical voice. The Wizard was discovered to be nothing but a collection of my own thoughts, strong desires, and an innocent amalgamation of false identities. I can never un-see what was seen.

Without the work of healing the trauma present in the body, the gift of awakening goes back to sleep, in a manner of speaking. Staying awake is the work of lifetimes.

PART V:

CONCLUSION

"You are needed, and now is your time."

—LEE HARRIS AND THE ZS

10

FATE AND FREE WILL

———

"A birth chart is a rich, living statement, full of insights, guidelines, and warnings. It describes not a static fate but a flowing life pattern, full of options and risks."

—STEVEN FORREST, "THE INNER SKY"

BACK AT BASECAMP

Let's review the territory we've covered. We were at basecamp Planet Earth in the Introduction, where you received an overview of the journey ahead and the tools we would use. The next chapters toured us through the solar system with stops at each of the nine major planetary worlds. Each of the nine planets' paths of evolution offered here are in themselves complete paths on their own. Taken together, they can guide our collective evolution. We are now back at basecamp ready to integrate all that we have seen and encountered.

Just as mythology needs a pantheon of gods and goddesses to represent the many archetypes and ways of being, reality needs a diversity of possible paths of evolution. We are united in spirit, yes, but we are a vast spectrum of individual expressions. The planets give us some basic possibilities to work with, much like the color spectrum lays out the human eye's perception of the complete array of colors.

From within that planetary spectrum of colors come infinite hues as you mix them. Mix a little Jupiter in with Mercury and you have a wholly new possible path than either Jupiter or Mercury could produce alone. On the canvas of consciousness, swirling watercolors form fluid images, both during creation and as they dry.

Can the colors continue to shift once they have dried? Yes, just add the water of awareness, inspiration, and free will. This chapter will explain how our free will interacts with our fate to create our destiny.

COSMIC ACCOUNTING

Nobody likes learning from their accountant that they owe taxes at the end of the tax year. But at some point in our growing up, we accept the unpleasant reality and either learn enough about tax law to keep ourselves financially on track or hire an accountant to give us solid advice. Our relationship with karma and astrology is similar.

ACCOUNTANTS AND ASTROLOGERS—FUN PARALLELS:
1. Both have access to aspects of your life you don't share with most people.
2. Both help you understand a specialized kind of "balance sheet" in your life.

3. Both use computations that require just a tiny bit of specialized know-how that you can easily learn yourself. However, if you don't have the time or inclination to learn the laws and keep up to date on new developments, it is advisable to consult a specialist.
4. Both sometimes give us good news and sometimes give us bad news.
5. Many of us will never know how well-versed or hard-working they are until they assist us through an audit or season of karma.

That is why it is important you work with scrupulous, trustworthy, smart, knowledgeable, hardworking accountants and astrologers who you vibe with.

THE BIRTH CHART AS A MAP OF KARMA

Besides being an absolutely exquisite representation of the geometric dance taking place in the cosmos at the moment of your birth, the *astrological birth chart* also functions as a kind of map of your karma. For some readers this might be an uneasy concept to encounter, so I hope to assuage those concerns a bit, being your trusted astrologer (or cosmic accountant) at the moment.

Karma is an odious concept to our "I create my own destiny" way of thinking. But what if those two conceptual frameworks—karma and free will—are not mutually exclusive? Could it be possible that we are both living out our karma *and* creating our own destiny?

DO I HAVE TO BELIEVE IN KARMA
AND REINCARNATION FOR THIS BOOK TO BE OF USE TO ME?

The concepts of karma and reincarnation provide the engine for any evolutionary potential that can be unlocked by the chart. The idea that consciousness cycles inside life forms until it evolves into full recognition of its true identity as the source of all that is, is foundational to Vedic Astrology.

That said, if you don't buy the idea of reincarnation, don't worry. I kind of don't either. Let me explain.

Sometime in my twenties in a meditation, I had a visceral experience about the nature of Time. I felt how Time is not linear. I felt how all of Time exists right now. Set against this backdrop, all forms of sentient life bear "resonance" with other sentient life forms, in much the same way an "A" note played on one guitar will have a nearby guitar resonate at the same 440 hz frequency. In that meditation, I experienced that our idea of reincarnation is nothing more than "resonance" between life forms across our limited understanding of Time.

How we choose to understand what pulls us toward our most full, authentic expression is an individual discovery. Not everyone understands this pull as explained by a series of lifetimes in which we do it better until we get it right. Some choose to see this process as the human genome, evolving itself.

HIGHER OCTAVE DNA

The birth chart can be seen as a kind of higher octave of our DNA—the *meta*-physical facet of the gene pool we inherit and the propensity we have toward expressing both the strengths and traumatic burdens of our lineages.

The scientific field of genetics has a relatively young and growing focus called epigenetics, which is defined by Carrie Deans and Keith Maggert in their National Center for Biotechnology Information 2015 article as "the study of phenomena and mechanisms that cause chromosome-bound, heritable changes to gene expression that are not dependent on changes to DNA sequence."

In other words, how you respond to your environment can be inherited, just as much as a predetermined characteristic, like eye color, can be inherited. Eye color is passed along through the DNA sequence. Your environmental responses are not passed along in the DNA sequence but are heritable, nonetheless. For instance, my propensity to eat every last bite on my plate even if I'm full might be motivated by ancestral responses to periods of starvation they endured.

And even within all that inherited material (as laid out in the genome and the epigenome), as humans, *we adapt*, which is not, as far as we know, predetermined. In an article from 2018 titled "Intergenerational Transmission of Trauma Effects: Putative Role of Epigenetic Mechanisms," Rachel Yehuda and Amy Lehrner conclude that "the principle of epigenetic plasticity implies that changes to the epigenome might reset when the environmental insults are no longer present, or when we have changed sufficiently to address environmental challenges in a new way. It is the ability to flexibly respond to environmental stimuli that is fundamentally adaptive and the basis of human resilience." Free will, anyone?

HOW DOES FREE WILL IMPACT THE BIRTH CHART?

We can't appreciate the stunning magnificence of our free will until we understand what we come into life preprogrammed with. Science provides a basis of understanding on a technical level, and now we move into viewing what is predetermined through the lens of astrology.

What most of the astrological literature written until this point hasn't yet been able to take into account is the important context that *karma has its roots in trauma.*

In his book, *Healing Collective Trauma,* Thomas Hübl writes:

> The "past" is unintegrated history. It is that content of our story, personal and collective, that has been buried in shadow, the dark lakes of the unconscious interior, and thereby made into karma, forced to surface again and again in our exterior world. Unintegrated, unconscious past is destiny. It becomes a false future projected into tomorrow, built of repetition, preprogrammed by our unawakened aspect. It is like taking the road behind us, placing it in front of us, and calling it the "future."

> What we have called "karma" or "shadow" may, today, be called "trauma," since the effects of trauma propagate as dissociated and denied energies, frozen in shadow, bound to repeat. Trauma creates incoherence, fracturing us from ourselves and separating us from others. Its broken memories resurface repeatedly through exterior eruptions that are not directed by free will but by that part of the self that is held in darkness.

In Chapter Nine, where I cover Ketu's evolutionary path, we delved more specifically into working with trauma, bringing presence to this darkness.

Where trauma is not so thick or intractable, we as humans have an enormous amount of free will to work with in order to evolve. Free will is the X Factor to an Agent of Evolution—that catalyzing aspect of our own consciousness that says "yes" to growth and development in all its forms—emotional, physical, intellectual, ethical, spiritual—even when it's not pleasant, convenient, or profitable.

Adaptations to our changing environment come about through our free will. In other words, adaptations are not destiny—they are choice. For example, free will is what we employ anytime we are changing a habit. Let's say I have a bad habit of interrupting people, and I intentionally decide I want to stop doing that. By even making that choice, I have employed my free will. And then, moment by moment, it is my free will that allows me to choose to remember my choice and listen, rather than interrupt.

Though the birth chart mostly shows that type of karma which can't be changed, how we respond to that unchangeable karma and what karma we create for our future is entirely in our control. We ourselves truly author what will happen in our future.

THE THREE TYPES OF KARMA

Jyotish, or Vedic Astrology, was meant to be practical. It was developed by evolved beings who saw a need to help guide us in our earthly existence, because let's face it—life is bewildering sometimes. These ancient seers observed patterns and put pieces of wisdom into concepts from which we can benefit.

I have grown to trust this beautiful wisdom tradition and to lean into its conceptual frameworks, because they are practical, helpful, and lend peace of mind.

One such framework is the Vedic principle outlining three distinct types of karma: The kind that cannot be changed, like being born with brown eyes; the kind that can be changed, like having a fear of crowded places; and the kind we are creating right now with our thoughts and actions in response to all the situations we find ourselves in.

Like I often do when I need some insight or clarification on Vedic Astrology, I called my Vedic Astrology teacher, James Kelleher, to ask him about karma. He has a knack for explaining confusing concepts in simple ways.

"The Vedic view of cosmology is one of an expanding and contracting universe, you know?" is his response to my question about whether the Vedic seers ever predicted we would annihilate ourselves. (I couldn't resist. When do you ever get to ask questions like this with a straight face, except of your astrology teacher?) "Brahma creates the universe. Vishnu maintains the universe while it's in existence. Shiva collapses the universe at the end of time."

Okay, so no destruction is ever total, because evolution is cyclical, circular. There's no end point or final stage of enlightenment human life is reaching for. Evolution is not a straight line, it is a spiral.

James then turned to explaining the three types of karma:

1. Sanchita karma
2. Prarabdha karma
3. Kriyamana karma and Agama karma

"When you talk about karma, you've got Sanchita karma, which we can think of as the storehouse of karma in the background—all the karmas you've accumulated from your past life and many, many past lives. Sanchita would be the storehouse of karma that you have accumulated over time. And then Prarabdha karma is the one little pile of karma that is put on your plate for this lifetime. Luckily, life is compassionate, and it doesn't make you go through the whole [storehouse of karma] all at once. It gives you only an amount you can take. And so, it gives you one little plateful—that's your Prarabdha karma; it's on your plate."

Bite-size. Nice.

"Now, Prarabdha Karma has three intensities—you know, mama bear, baby bear, papa bear." *Yup. This I know from personal experience.* "It can be intense, like papa bear, or it can be medium like mama bear, or it can be mild, like baby bear. If it's intense, it's really tough to change it. If it's medium, you have to make some effort, but you can change it. And if it's mild, then you can just do whatever you want with your free will. So, that's Prarabdha karma."

I know James's storytelling style well enough to know he's about to arrive at the juicy stuff. "Now, Kriyamana karma is the karma of free will. And here, really, we're lumping together two types of karma: Kriyamana karma and Agama karma. Kriyamana karma is the free will that you put into motion, that you actually *do*. And Agama karma would be your plans to do it. So, when you sit down and you visualize that you want to make a million dollars, that's Agama karma. You're saying, 'I don't have any money. I've heard that if I have positive thinking, I will be able to make more money. So, I'm going to visualize it, and I'm going to do affirmations, and I'm going to think about and plan for it.' That's Agama karma. It's very important and really helpful. And then if I put it into motion and actually act on my plan, then that's Kriyamana karma—exerting free will."

Hallelujah! I knew I wasn't just a walking, talking karma machine!

"And the important thing here is, that from a practical level, it gives you the clarity and the understanding of this fate versus free will thing. That's the whole point of this way of describing the theory of karma. It's that, yes, we do have to deal with the momentum of what we set in motion in the past. There's no way around it: the stuff that's on our plate in this lifetime, we've got to deal with," James explains.

"But on the other side of it," he continues, "we have free will. And we can exert that free will. And sometimes it's a little harder, because the karma that comes down is intense. Sometimes it's easy. But you know, if you plan and then you enact your plans, by virtue of your will, it will work. You'll be able to offset and mitigate your karma."

Whew! Massive sigh of relief.

AGENTS OF EVOLUTION, TAKE HEART

"I wish it need not have happened in my time," said Frodo. "So do I," said Gandalf, "and so do all who live to see such times. But that is not for them to decide. All we have to decide is what to do with the time that is given us."

—J. R. R. TOLKIEN

Our evolution is inevitable. Whether we are in a particularly dense period of human history where things seem to be devolving or we are in an enlightened age, or whether we keep making horrible personal choices or great choices, the sages from India tell us we are following *the cyclic nature of evolution.* So, from this vantage point, we can breathe easier knowing we are ultimately headed in the direction we intend to be going.

At the same time, if we want to do ourselves a favor and turn our collective human ship away from the iceberg we seem to be heading toward, we can. But we have to *choose* that other path and steer the ship in a different direction, together. It might seem like a daunting proposition, but this book aims to help you play your part in taking hold of that collective steering wheel by making different choices than the ones set out by your karma.

11

HOW TO BE AN AGENT OF EVOLUTION

———

"Reading is going toward something that is about to be, and no one yet knows what it will be."

—ITALO CALVINO, *IF ON A WINTER'S NIGHT A TRAVELER*

Back in 1988, a friend gave me my first astrology book called Astrology, Karma, and Transformation, *by Stephen Arroyo. The book captivated me, even though I was skeptical about astrology back then.*

I was working in New York City at Atlantic Records's recording studio in Columbus Circle as an assistant engineer with aspirations to score films. In the meantime, I wrote songs that were getting picked up by dance artists of the late eighties. I was living in a tiny, shared apartment in Brooklyn's "Red Hook"—a neighborhood that has since become gentrified, but back then was the perfect, seedy development ground for aspiring artists.

My post-college friends were a tight-knit bunch. There was an extended pack of us who all attended Berklee College of Music in Boston and had moved to NYC around the same time. Many of us lived in the same neighborhood in Red Hook; four of the seven of us were in my tiny apartment. We were all musicians, audio engineers, and songwriters, which back then was a reliably open-minded set, ready to take on deep philosophical conversation at breakfast over our Bustello coffee made in the espresso maker, with baguette and fresh mozzarella from the Italian market a couple blocks down. Looking back, I know I was lucky to be among such freewheeling people. They provided a fertile environment for me to begin remembering my astrological heritage.

Music, like astrology, requires a huge amount of dedication and, sometimes, sacrifice. It's as if I developed my dedication to craft among the cousins of astrologers. Music and astrology are not very different in the end. You pick up where you left off last lifetime and keep developing the craft.

I'm convinced my relationship with astrology didn't begin in this lifetime. Whether I had ancestors somewhere down the line who made a great study of it, or whether I myself have been an astrologer in previous lives, I know I came into this life with a certain amount of familiarity with the language. When I opened that first astrology book, I took to it like a duck to water.

I wanted more. I couldn't stop reading. As fate would have it, the most fabulous bookstore—a place called Weiser's in midtown Manhattan's east side—was readily accessible to me. This bookstore was the Hogwarts of its day. Any title on any kind of esoterica was to be found there, and all the strange wizards and witches of Manhattan frequented the place, lurking about *the aisles or having conversations on the sidewalk outside. It wasn't just a place to buy books. It was a place to hobnob with others much more experienced, to learn, and to test your craft.*

The young astrologers of today have so much available to them as virtual, classrooms and communities explode. I hope this book might be a link in the chain to their astrological heritage for some of them.

Being tethered to the stars has always been, for me, a way of connecting to "home," or a sense of place, especially since my parents are both immigrants to the United States, where I was born. Never feeling I belonged anywhere I lived or traveled, my home has always been the stars. And in my funny cosmic belonging, I hope I am bringing to you, my reader, a sense of possibility that all of us on Earth belong to Earth and to the stars—that we are all a part of that Vastness. That this is what unites us.

It was the year 2020 that sealed the deal for me. After working in the music industry in the late 1980s and early nineties, I spent the next few decades working in publications, and in graphic and multimedia design, and most recently in video and film. Over thirty years after opening my first astrology book, what was probably obvious to others finally became apparent to me. Somewhat reluctantly and surreptitiously practicing astrology professionally since 2006, I finally had the courage to turn to a full-time astrology practice again and be public about it in 2018. As 2020 progressed and I sat in session after session with my clients, watching my inner sense of what we were all about to experience be confirmed, the reality of my calling was finally irrefutable to me.

WHICH PLANET ARE YOU FROM?

In Vedic Astrology, we look at the degrees of each planet in its sign to determine how close, so to speak, that planet is to our *Soul*'s essential expression. (With thirty degrees to each of the twelve signs making up the three-hundred sixty degrees of the zodiac, each planet, star, or celestial body can be mapped onto that three-hundred sixty degree backdrop.) The planet with highest degree tends to be the planet closest to your Soul's most essential design. You can think of this planet as the planet you're "from."

The planet sitting at the highest degree claims the unique status of being your "Atmakaraka," or significator of the Soul. (Not to be confused with your essential *self* as expressed in this lifetime, which is represented by your Sun.) Focusing on this one planet's path of evolution in your own life will yield the fruits of all planets' paths of evolution, because you are tending the specific expression your Soul naturally embodies, and in doing that one piece you do so well, you help us evolve as a collective.

Your Atmakaraka may be surprising to you. Mine was to me; Mars was not what I expected, but there it is in my chart—at twenty-seven degrees of Libra, Mars is the planet with the highest degrees inside the sign he occupies. Mars is without question the planet whose path of evolution yields the biggest fruits for me when I truly align with it.

Unfortunately, without astrology software, it's hard to know this simple calculation of which planet has the highest number of degrees in any sign in the *sidereal zodiac* in your *Vedic* astrological birth chart. In the absence of knowing this information, pick the planet whose chapter you are naturally drawn to and focus on the competencies of that planet. Maybe your body came alive while reading one of the chapters; maybe you received a sign in the outer world after reading one of the chapters; or maybe you had a dream that related to one of the chapters. Open your awareness to these subtle cues from your life. As you start paying attention to them, these cues will become as real to you as if you were following an actual bread crumb trail.

Once you have a solid feeling about which of the planets you would like to focus on, make a commitment to being shown what kind of competency your own evolution requires. The core competencies of each planet's path of evolution written about here are primary suggestions. Let them be a jumping off point for your own discovery.

Each planet's competencies are meant to be practiced. Just like learning to play an instrument, it might take time to develop some facility in that domain, and you have to be committed to the repetition in order to develop your *chops*. Keep a journal and record your insights as you practice. Come back to these pages and read them again. There are no shortcuts. Mastery requires consistent repetition.

Now that you've explored all the chapters, try some of the writing prompts again. They are meant to be a starting point for deeper self-exploration within that planet's path of evolution. A guidebook to discovery. Work with the prompts. Play with them. Allow them to spur you onward. Let the whole universe conspire to help you find your true path. Listen to the signs you get from life and the natural world.

PARTNERING WITH THE NATURAL WORLD

My first true "familiar" was a tiny screech owl. He lived in a tree next to a bustling playground by the house where I lived and did readings. My then-husband would see this adorable little fluff bucket on his way to work each morning. I would see him on evening walks. We affectionately referred to him as Igor.

Before I began readings in those days, I had an elaborate ritual that helped me slip below the waves of the mind—a critical preparation for successful readings. As part of this ritual, I would tune into the Earth around my home, the trees and plant life, the creek down the hill, and all the creatures in my little micro-region. I would visit Igor in this state. He became a sort of ally in the work, much in the way an animal "familiar" supports a healer, by holding a kind of ceremonial safe space in a parallel realm to the waking world.

Igor's presence in the sessions was palpable, reliable, and even critical. On the rare occasion I would forget to let Igor know I was stepping into session, the session would "be off" in some way—I might have trouble accessing information, or I might somehow mix up the session time, or, horror of horrors, type in the wrong birth data.

I would sometimes hear screech owl calls lying in bed at night, and those calls always delivered messages. Often the messages were simple commentaries on a personal problem I was experiencing; sometimes they were a "heads up" on something about to transpire in the days to come.

After a couple years of partnership with Igor in the readings, the city cut down the tree in which Igor roosted, and Igor was no longer to be found. He visited me in a dream and let me know his time on Earth was up and to stay open to finding a new familiar. He also let me know my then husband and I would be moving soon. Sure enough, we found a new home shortly after that.

Partnering with the natural world is exquisitely simple. Take a minute and sense into the natural world beneath your feet, above your head, around you on all sides. What is it saying to you, *right now*?

If this way of being is new to you, play with it. It will yield riches beyond your wildest imagination.

TWELVE ATTITUDES WORTH CULTIVATING FOR AGENTS OF EVOLUTION

Being an Agent of Evolution requires us all to move outside our comfort zone a bit. We have to stretch ourselves and do things we are not necessarily accustomed to doing, see things in ways we are not necessarily used to seeing, and apprehend things in ways that can destabilize our worldviews. Making change is as much an inward journey as an outward one.

As our lives hurtle into the future with great speed, I propose to all Agents of Evolution twelve attitudes worth cultivating. Consider these attitudes as signposts inspired by the planets:

1. See things as they are. Resist the urge to believe your thoughts about What Is. Witness as neutrally as possible.
2. Tell the truth. This sounds simpler than it is in practice. There are all sorts of good reasons why we don't tell the truth. But truth liberates.

3. Surf the unknown. Surfing is fun!
4. Allow seemingly contradictory truths to exist simultaneously. We are in a period of human history where many timelines are being lived out side by side. What is true for one person, or in one moment, may not be true for another person, or in another moment. This is not a problem, though our minds have not fully developed the capacity yet to allow for this level of complexity.
5. Follow the somatic awakening of your body. Your body will cue you on next movements. You need your body to come along with you. It is not possible to do any of this without your body. Go only as fast as your body can integrate.
6. Be a transformative catalyst in groups. You don't have to do anything special to be a transformative catalyst. Just show up, be yourself, and have the intention to hold a space for transformation. Showing up organically and authentically will catalyze processes of transformation. Be in your vulnerability and allow the processes to unfold as they will.
7. Cultivate beginner's mind. Approach every circumstance, each moment, anew. Beginner's mind is a precept from the Zen tradition popularized in the West by Shunryu Suzuki's publication of *Zen Mind, Beginner's Mind*.
8. Give back to life rather than being transactional or extractive. Begin to value and find the joy in the exchange between you and every living being, understanding that this benefits them as well as you.
9. Strive for interdependence within the group, rather than artificially adhering to self-reliance. You will not get far on your own. There was a time for that in human history. This is not that time anymore.

10. Cultivate forgiveness. Easier said than done. This is an ongoing practice, and the benefits are enormous. Forgiveness of others starts with forgiving ourselves, which is possibly the hardest part. Forgiveness frees up our life energy for heightened creative living.

11. Honor and protect the earth as the source of our existence. This requires a reeducation of our Western mind, values, and orientation. If you are reading this book, you are probably already exposed to the work required to undo centuries of colonizer mindset.

12. Recognize your place in the circle of life and act for the benefit of previous generations and the ones to come. Right size yourself by always being aware of your actions' reverberations extending out first to your biological lineages, forward and backward, and then to each of the communities in which you participate.

RESOURCES

Do you ever pick up a book and turn to a random page, seeing if it has a message for you? If not, I encourage you to try it. This is a valid form of *divination*. In fact, try it with this book from time to time as a way of reminding yourself of the evolutionary competencies.

Knowing that repetition is required for mastery, read the chapters that are important to you more than once. You will receive different messages on a second, third, or fourth read. You may also benefit from visiting these pages at different milestones in your life, or in a period of transition or hardship.

The writing prompts you read during the chapters are compiled in an appendix for you to refer to as you continue sharpening your awareness of yourself. Your answers may change at different stages of your life.

If you are interested in pursuing astrology further, thumb through the resources appendix and see what calls out to you. Also listed there are resources for further exploring trauma healing work and transformative justice work.

ON BECOMING A GOOD ANCESTOR

"We ourselves shall be loved for awhile and forgotten. But the love will have been enough; all those impulses of love return to the love that made them. Even memory is not necessary for love. There is a land of the living and a land of the dead and the bridge is love, the only survival, the only meaning."

—THORNTON WILDER, THE BRIDGE OF SAN LUIS REY

We are heading into a period of unprecedented, radical, accelerated change on planet Earth. You may at times feel utterly daunted by what our collective transition is requiring of you, and at other times feel so incredibly grateful to be alive to witness it. That is perfectly normal.

There is no guarantee that we will survive as a species. But I feel deeply certain of our Soul's continuation in some form after we slip out of our bodies. The pain and heartache of our existence, as well as its little joys and triumphs, are part of life getting to experience itself. Beyond that, what is awake and aware does not die. And it is that primordial Spirit to which we return.

Wouldn't it be more fun to live this life we've been given to the fullest, aspiring to the stars? I see many great beings doing this and have attempted to share a few examples with you. I invite you into a sense of wonder and possibility: What is the most magical world our imaginations can dream up? As we answer life's call, we become good ancestors, leaving the world a better place for the ones to come after you and I are gone.

APPENDIX

APPENDIX

GLOSSARY

PREFACE

Chart rectification: An astrological technique of sifting through timing data and matching that data to the actual life of the entity to determine the correct time of birth.

Dharma: A primary concept defined differently by different spiritual traditions. In the way "dharma" is used in this book, it can be defined as the arrangement inherent in reality and each being's place within it. I like to explain it this way: "The dharma of a rose is to have a fragrance of a rose. The dharma of a gardenia is to have the fragrance of a gardenia. A rose cannot have the fragrance of a gardenia, or vice versa. And why would they want to?"

Jyotish: A Sanskrit word meaning "the science of light." Also called Vedic Astrology, because the profound and mathematically sophisticated system is classified as an *upaveda*, or a body of knowledge auxiliary to the Vedas, the ancient scriptures of India.

"Jyotish describes the planetary patterns at the time of our birth and can give us valuable clues to understanding our life's journey. Through careful analysis of these cosmic influences, Jyotish can help us to realistically evaluate our strengths and challenges in order to optimize our full potential. By forecasting the changing trends and periods of our lives, Jyotish can also enable us to make more evolutionary choices. It offers practical remedial measures to alleviate areas of difficulty, giving us the confidence to manifest our true destiny and create success, happiness, and harmony on all levels." (BecVar, 2013)

Jyotishi: One who practices Jyotish.

Karma: The principle that for every action there is an equal and opposite reaction. Stated differently, what you sow, you reap.

Mundane Astrology: Also known as political astrology. The application of astrology to world affairs and world events, taking its name from the Latin word *Mundus*, meaning "the World."

INTRODUCTION

Archetype: Many academic definitions exist for this concept. Here is the definition that matches the usage of this concept in this book: A primary theme in human experience, often represented in the arts and mythologies of cultures; a recurring character construct that shows specific responses to the environment around them.

Mahatma: A Sanskrit word meaning "great being" or "great Soul." (Feuerstein, 2021)

Navagraha: A Sanskrit combination word—*nava* means nine, *graha* means planet. (Dalal, 2010)

Rishi: A Sanskrit word meaning "seer," or "sage." (Feuerstein, 2021)

CHAPTER 1: THE SUN
Sangha: A community who share values and support one another.

CHAPTER 3: MERCURY
Mindfulness: Thich Nhat Hanh often describes mindfulness as: "Being aware of what is happening inside and around you in the present moment." The Thich Nhat Hanh Foundation explains that "through mindfulness, we can learn to live happily in the present moment—as a way to truly develop peace, both in one's self and in the world. We see mindfulness as part of a path, beyond a tool or technique, that requires training and practice. It can be talked about in words, but its true transformative power is felt only when experienced firsthand." (Thich Nhat Hanh Foundation, 2021)

Neurodecolonization: An antidote to the ongoing effects of colonization that addresses the nervous system of the person and communities affected, "combining mindfulness approaches with traditional and contemporary secular and sacred contemplative practices to replace negative patterns of thought, emotion, and behavior with healthy, productive ones." (Yellowbird, 2021)

CHAPTER 4: VENUS

Commons: Cultural and natural resources accessible to everyone, held in common (not privately owned)—such as the air, water, and a habitable Earth—that collectives manage for the benefit of all. (Basu, 2017)

Eros: The way the term eros is being used in the Venus chapter is similar to the way it is used in *The Power of Divine Eros*, by Karen Johnson and A. H. Almaas: Eros is "the inherent energy of the zest and sparkle of our life force." Johnson and Almaas draw the parallel between eros/the erotic and the sexual, showing how they are related but not the same. They also unpack how the erotic and the divine are not separate and how the passionate aliveness of our relationships can be a gateway to wholeness.

CHAPTER 5: MARS

Ayurveda: Ancient healing science from India, originating more than five thousand years ago, passed on in an oral tradition from teacher to student over thousands of years. In Sanskrit, Ayurveda means "the Science of Life." (Lad, 2006)

CHAPTER 6: JUPITER

Aspect (astrological): A geometric relationship between two points in a chart. Different astrological aspects carry different astrological significance.

Natal: Relating to the place or time of one's birth.

Natal chart (a.k.a. birth chart): A diagram of the planets' positions at the exact moment of one's birth, from the viewpoint of the place they were born.

Natal planet: The position of a planet at the moment of one's birth, from the viewpoint of the place they were born.

Transit (astrological): A transit occurs when a natal planet is aspected by any planet in its current course.

CHAPTER 8: RAHU

Aikido: A Japanese martial art originally developed by Morihei Ueshiba, whose primary goal is to achieve victory over oneself rather than cultivate aggression. Aikido translates as "the way of unifying with life energy." (Saotome, 1989)

Tantra/Tantric: *"Like many Sanskrit words, Tantra has multiple meanings, but it is often translated as 'the wisdom that saves.' Despite its reputation as an esoteric practice, its teachings were originally intended for everyday people who, centuries ago, contended with relatable challenges. Tantra is relevant now because it was—and remains—a path in which every experience of life is a potential doorway to liberation. Tantric practice gives both worldly success and spiritual liberation, and shows you how ecstasy can be found even in the midst of confusion and discomfort."*

—SALLY KEMPTON (KEMPTON, 2021)

CHAPTER 9: KETU
Spiritual bypass: The use of spiritual practices and beliefs to avoid dealing with our painful feelings, unresolved wounds, and developmental needs. (Masters, 2013)

CHAPTER 10: FATE AND FREE WILL
Astrological birth chart (a.k.a. natal chart): An astronomical diagram of the heavens representing the moment of your birth.

Brahma: God in his aspect as creator. Part of the Hindu trinity. (Kelleher, 2006)

Vishnu: Preserver of the universe. Part of the Hindu trinity. (Kelleher, 2006)

Shiva: The Absolute; the Supreme Reality. Dissolver of the universe. Part of the Hindu trinity. (Kelleher, 2006)

"From a Tantric perspective, the inner masculine—Shiva—is the source of consciousness, awareness. But in order to act, to stir, he must take energy from the inner feminine."

—SALLY KEMPTON (KEMPTON, 2013)

CHAPTER 11: HOW TO BE AN AGENT OF EVOLUTION
Divination: Noticing your own inner wisdom reflected back to you by interpreting the signs given by something outside your own mind.

Sidereal Zodiac: Zodiac used in Vedic Astrology. (Kelleher, 2006) A system of calculating horoscopes on the backdrop of fixed stars (as distinguished from the Tropical Zodiac used by Western Astrology which calculates horoscopes differently.)

Vedic birth chart (a.k.a. Vedic horoscope): Your Vedic birth chart is calculated differently than your Western Astrology birth chart. All placements in your Vedic birth chart will be about twenty-four degrees earlier in the zodiac than in your Western birth chart. Though there are websites that will calculate your Vedic birth chart for free, the best way to engage with your Vedic birth chart is to consult a Vedic astrologer. If you don't want a full reading, tell them you're interested in knowing your *Atmakaraka* (pronounced AHT•muh KA•ruh•kuh).

WRITING PROMPTS

The writing prompts from the chapters are reprinted for you as a collection so you can easily come back to them. You may discover something new each time you work with these prompts.

THE SUN

Try your own hand at authoring a new narrative in this fun, simple way. First, call to mind a particular world crisis. If the world crisis were a villain, what kind of villain would it be? Picture this villain in your mind's eye.

Now set your timer for five minutes and write the narrative for a comic book, creating a superhero that comes in to battle that villain. What superpowers do they have? Who are their allies? What early wounds have they healed revealing their great strength and uniquely positioning them to vanquish the villain?

THE MOON

All Moon work begins with being intimately familiar with your inner emotional landscape. The practice of writing or journaling often works to help you explore and discover that terrain. Try setting a timer for ten minutes and answering this question:

What does my feeling body want to tell me today?

Put pen to paper and don't stop. Write gibberish if you get stuck. Just write whatever comes to your mind. Once the ten minutes are up, put away what you've written and revisit it a little later in the day. You might be able to connect some dots for yourself.

MERCURY

The benefit of undoing structures in our brains and nervous systems is that we free ourselves up to create new worlds that don't replicate the old dysfunctions. What does your ideal world look like?

Write the manifesto for your utopia. Set a timer for ten minutes. You can use this sentence stem to get you started: In my utopia, we believe _____.

VENUS

Venus wants us to feel good. To approach any of Venus's evolutionary goals, we'll want to start with what brings us joy. Try these writing prompts in the order suggested to remind yourself that evolving Venus does not require giving up what you love. On the contrary, a collectively oriented Venus gets us closer to what really makes our hearts happy, delighted, and fulfilled.

First:

Write about **the life you dream of living**, five years from now. Sketch a visual representation of this dream life—it could be a drawing, a diagram, a bunch of words floating on the page, a cartoon. . . Draw an iconic form of your visual representation on a Sticky note and put it on your laptop. Realize that you are creating a blueprint for the universe to build from—so let your enthusiasm bubble up! Venus is magnetized by your enthusiasm.

Second:

Write about **the world you dream of inhabiting**, five years from now. Sketch a visual representation of this world. Draw an iconic form of that world on a Sticky note and put it next to your personal life dream icon Sticky note on your laptop. Feel the relationship between them every time you look at them.

MARS

Take a minute and consider Joanna Macy's call to action— shifting from an industrial growth society to a life-sustaining civilization. How do you recruit *your* fighting spirit toward this worthy goal? Complete this sentence stem to find out:

If I were able to marshal all the energy available to me, the one thing I would do for the sake of my world is _____.

(This writing prompt is borrowed from Joanna Macy. She introduces "open sentences" like this one in her workshops as a form of group practice. For more on Joanna Macy, and for more on practicing with open sentences, please visit the Resources and Notes in the appendix.)

JUPITER

Do you want to view the glass as half empty (nature as competitive) or half full (nature as collaborative; nature as a web of gifts; the universe as benevolent)? What do you think Jupiter would do?

If I lived in a world where all my basic needs were met by the world around me, what gift would I be free to offer the world?

SATURN

Call to mind a situation you have a hard time accepting.

Now complete this writing prompt:

By accepting this situation, I am afraid that _____.

Read your statement out loud, and then read the following out loud:

I do not have to approve of this situation. I do not have to love the harm or the one creating the harm. Accepting does not mean I collapse into ineffectiveness, nor does it mean I stop working to change the situation. Accepting the situation means I get my life energy back.

RAHU

One way to work with Rahu is to spend time actively feeling our unlimited potential for experience. In expanding our identity to include everything, we loosen the chokehold Rahu has on us. (If I *am* everything, I don't need to go anywhere to experience anything. I can stay right where I am because all of life is within *me*.) This might feel conceptual at first. Allow yourself to play with it, and over time it will become a lived experience. Let this writing prompt help you discover the truth that "I am one with everything":

At the top of a blank page, write, "This Too, This Too Am I."

Set a timer for one minute. You will be writing a list of things—absolutely anything that comes to mind—the only qualification for what you write is that it must be a noun (e.g., glass, table, tree, sparkling diamond, lazy Sunday afternoon, blizzard, toxic femininity, bodacious taco, washed-up minstrel, long and winding river finding its way to the ocean, part-time genius). Write each new thing on a new line. Both short and long lines are fine.

When you are done writing the list, read the list out loud to yourself, putting "I am a(n)" before each line.

After you have read your own list, you may want to revisit Thich Nhat Hanh's poem, "Please Call Me by My True Names."

KETU

Connecting with Ketu's aliases in your life can be a breadcrumb trail leading you to Ketu's deeper gifts.

Write a list of the blessings and burdens you have received from your ancestors—all the resources, personality traits, interests, fears, orientations, and anything else you think of that are their legacy to you. At the end of this list, thank your ancestors, somewhat like this: "Praise and blessings to my Ancestors. Thank you for the gift of life. Teach me how to embody your blessings, for all my relations. May you be at peace."

(This writing prompt is inspired by a prayer offered by Dr. Daniel Foor during an ancestral medicine training. Check the resources section for more information on ancestor reverence ritual.)

RESOURCES

———

TO LEARN MORE ABOUT ASTROLOGY, START HERE:

Western Astrology:

The Mountain Astrologer Magazine
mountainastrologer.com

Astrology University
astrologyuniversity.com

The Astrology Podcast
theastrologypodcast.com

Kepler College
keplercollege.org

The Organization for Professional Astrology (OPA)
opaastrology.org

Association for Young Astrologers (AYA)
youngastrologers.org

New Paradigm Astrology
newparadigmastrology.com

<u>Western Evolutionary Astrology:</u>

Steven Forrest
The Inner Sky
forrestastrology.com

Jeffrey Greene
Structure of the Soul
schoolofevolutionaryastrology.com

<u>Vedic Astrology (Jyotish):</u>

James Kelleher, Sierra Institute of Vedic Studies
Path of Light, Volumes I & II
jameskelleher.com

Dr. David Frawley, American Institute of Vedic Studies
Astrology of the Seers
vedanet.com

Hart DeFouw and Robert Svoboda
Light on Life: An Introduction to the Astrology of India

TO LEARN MORE ABOUT ANIMISM, START HERE:
The best way to learn about animism is to visit the grand-mothers in your region and see what they are willing to share with you. Seek out the indigenous grandmothers, approach them with sincerity, humility, and good humor, and see if they will teach you.

<u>Scholars on Animism</u>

Dr. Daniel Foor
Ancestral Medicine: Rituals for Personal and Family Healing

Graham Harvey
Animism: Respecting the Living World

Keith Basso
Wisdom Sits in Places

**TO LEARN MORE ABOUT ANCESTOR REVERENCE PRACTICE,
START HERE:**

Dr. Daniel Foor
Ancestral Medicine: Rituals for Personal and Family Healing
ancestralmedicine.org

TO LEARN MORE ABOUT HEALING TRAUMA, START HERE:
Peter Levine
Waking the Tiger: Healing Trauma

Bessel Van der Kolk
The Body Keeps the Score

Thomas Hübl
Healing Collective Trauma

Resmaa Menakem
My Grandmother's Hands

TO EXPLORE TRANSFORMATIVE JUSTICE, START HERE:
All books by adrienne marie brown, especially:
Emergent Strategy: Shaping Change, Changing Worlds
*Holding Change: The Way of Emergent Strategy Facilitation
and Mediation*

TO LEARN MORE ABOUT HUMANITY'S "GREAT TRANSITION,"
START HERE:

Duane and Coleen Elgin, Choosing Earth Project:
Book: *Choosing Earth*, by Duane Elgin
Documentary Film: choosingearth.org/video, by Coleen
Elgin
choosingearth.org

MORE "OPEN SENTENCES"
AND OTHER PRACTICES FROM JOANNA MACY:

Joanna Macy, Work That Reconnects
workthatreconnects.org/resources/practices/

NOTES

PREFACE

"A Warning on Climate and the Risk of Societal Collapse." *The Guardian.* Letters. December 6, 2020. https://www.theguardian.com/environment/2020/dec/06/a-warning-on-climate-and-the-risk-of-societal-collapse.

Abram, David. *Becoming Animal: An Earthly Cosmology.* New York: Pantheon Books, 2010.

BecVar, Brent. "Introduction to Jyotish: Vedic Astrology." Chopra, Mind-Body Heath Articles. November 7, 2013. https://chopra.com/articles/introduction-to-jyotish-vedic-astrology.

Brennan, Chris, and Keiron Le Grice. "Jung on Synchronicity and the Mechanism for Astrology." March 16, 2018, Episode 148. In *The Astrology Podcast.* Podcast, MP3 audio, 2:38:54. https://theastrologypodcast.com/2018/03/16/jung-on-synchronicity-and-the-mechanism-for-astrology/.

Campion, Nicholas. *A History of Western Astrology, Volume 1: The Ancient and Classical Worlds.* London: Continuum, 2008.

Elgin, Duane. *Choosing Earth: Humanity's Great Transition to a Mature Planetary Civilization*. Woodacre: Self-published, 2020.

Foor, Daniel. "Animism and Earth Ritual." Ancestral Medicine. Accessed May 27, 2021. https://ancestralmedicine.org/animism/.

Forrest, Steven. *The Inner Sky*. Borrego Springs, CA: Seven Paws Press, Inc., 2012.

Jung, C. G. *Collected Works of C.G. Jung, Volume 15: Spirit in Man, Art, And Literature*. Princeton: Princeton University Press, 2014.

Kelleher, James. "Past World Predictions by JK on Corona Virus." March 20, 2020. Video, 21:18. https://youtu.be/dDHCOzqPVbk

O'Hara, Paul. "The Lost Science of the Stars." Unimed Living. Accessed June 29, 2021. https://www.unimedliving.com/science/our-celestial-home/the-lost-science-of-the-stars.html.

Tarnas, Richard. *Cosmos and Psyche: Intimations of a New World View*. New York: Viking Press, 2006.

INTRODUCTION

Atharva Veda. Ajmer, India: Śrīmatī Paropakārini Sabhā, 1974.

Dalal, Roshen. *Hinduism: An Alphabetical Guide*. India: Penguin Books, 2010.

Feuerstein, Georg. "200 Key Sanskrit Yoga Terms." *Yoga Journal*. August 28, 2007. https://www.yogajournal.com/yoga-101/200-key-sanskrit-yoga-terms/.

Frawley, David. "Planets in the Vedic Literature," *Indian Journal of History of Science* vol. 29, no. 4 (July 18, 1994): 495–496, 502. https://insa.nic.in/writereaddata/UpLoadedFiles/IJHS/Vol29_4_1_DFrawley.pdf.

CHAPTER 1: THE SUN

American Federation of Astrologers. "History of Astrology." Accessed May 24, 2021. https://www.astrologers.com/about/history.

Cipriani, Casey. "Watch: Ava DuVernay In Action Behind the Scenes of 'Selma.'" *IndieWire.* Accessed May 24, 2021. https://www.indiewire.com/2014/12/watch-ava-duvernay-in-action-behind-the-scenes-of-selma-66658/.

Goldberg, Emma. "Ava DuVernay's Fight for Change, Onscreen and Off." *The New York Times,* July 8, 2020. https://www.nytimes.com/2020/07/08/movies/director-ava-duvernay-movies-police-protests.html.

Integral Living Room. "The Evolution of the Integral We-Space: A Conversation with Ken Wilber." The Integral Living Room. July 27, 2013. http://www.integrallivingroom.com/the-evolution-of-the-integral-we-space-a-conversation-with-ken-wilber-2/.

Kofman, Fred. "Discovering Our True Nature." *Conscious Business: Transforming Your Workplace (and Yourself) by Changing the Way You Think, Act, and Communicate.* Accessed May 24, 2021. Audio, 5:17. https://www.soundstrue.com/products/conscious-business-1.

Moyers, Bill, and Joseph Campbell. *The Power of Myth.* New York: Knopf Doubleday Publishing Group, 2011.

Nhat Hanh, Thich. "The Next Buddha May Be a Sangha." *Inquiring Mind,* no. 2, Vol. 10 (Spring 1994). Accessed May 19, 2021. https://www.inquiringmind.com/article/1002_41_thich-nhat_hanh/.

The Aspen Institute. "Conversations with Great Leaders: Ava DuVernay and Damian Woetzel." Oct. 17, 2017. Video, 59:18. https://youtu.be/H8x4LWxgOt4.

CHAPTER 2: THE MOON

Castle, Elizabeth. "'The Original Gangster': The Life and Times of Red Power Activist Madonna Thunder Hawk." In *The Hidden 1970s: Histories of Radicalism*, edited by Dan Berger, 267–84. New Brunswick: Rutgers University Press, 2010. http://www.jstor.org/stable/j.ctt5hjb9s.19.

Castle, Elizabeth A., and Christina D. King, dir. *Warrior Women*. 2018. Vision Maker Media, Castle King LLC, ITVS. Viewed October 17, 2020, at the 2020 Bend Film Festival, online. https://www.warriorwomenfilm.com/synopsis.

Newman, Amie. "What the Standing Rock Resistance Can Teach Us About Reproductive Justice for Native American Women." *Our Bodies Ourselves*, December 8, 2016. https://www.our-bodiesourselves.org/2016/12/what-standing-rock-can-teach-us-about-reproductive-justice-for-native-american-women/.

Rootead Enrichment Center. Home page. Accessed May 24, 2021. https://www.rootead.org/.

United States Geological Survey (USGS). "The Water in You: Water and the Human Body." Water Science School. Accessed June 22, 2021. https://www.usgs.gov/special-topic/water-science-school/science/water-you-water-and-human-body?qt-science_center_objects=0#qt-science_center_objects.

CHAPTER 3: MERCURY

Baker, John Alec. *The Peregrine*. United States: New York Review Books, 2005.

Congress.gov. "Text — H.Res.109 — 116th Congress: Recognizing the Duty of the Federal Government to Create a Green New Deal." February 12, 2019. https://www.congress.gov/bill/116th-congress/house-resolution/109/text.

Edmonson, Katie, Emily Cochrane, and Lisa Friedman. "Liberal Freshmen Are Shaking the Capitol Just Days into the New Congress." *The New York Times.* January 6, 2019. https://www. nytimes.com/2019/01/06/us/politics/tlaib-aoc-new-congress. html.

Everytable. "About." Accessed June 27, 2021. https://www.everytable.com/about.

Foor, Daniel. "Boundaries, Consent, and Sacred Space." Practical Animism Online Course, Winter 2021. Q&A Call Transcript: Week 4. January 26, 2021.

Gawain, Shakti. *Creative Visualization: Use the Power of Your Imagination to Create What You Want in Your Life.* United States: New World Library, 2010.

Godin, Seth. "Even if It's not Graduation Week for You. . . " *Seth's Blog.* June 14, 2019. https://seths.blog/2019/06/writing-not-plastics-not-wall-street/.

Kaufer, Katrin, and Otto Scharmer. *Leading from the Emerging Future.* San Francisco: Berrett-Koehler Publishers, Inc., 2013. 146–151.

Keats, John. *The Letters of John Keats.* United Kingdom: Harvard University Press, 1958.

Mosher, Dave. "Alexandria Ocasio-Cortez, the 28-Year-Old Who Defeated a Powerful House Democrat, Has an Asteroid Named after Her—Here's Why." *Business Insider.* June 28, 2018. https:// www.businessinsider.com/alexandria-ocasio-cortez-asteroid-2018-6.

Scharmer, Otto, Peter Senge. *Theory U: Leading from the Future as It Emerges.* San Francisco: Berrett-Koehler Publishers, 2016.

Thich Nhat Hanh Foundation. "About Mindfulness." Homepage. Accessed June 28, 2021. https://thichnhathanhfoundation.org/.

Yellowbird, Michael. "About." Neurodecolonization and Indigenous Mindfulness. Accessed June 27, 2021. https://www.indigenousmindfulness.com/about.

United States House of Representatives. "Alexandria Ocasio-Cortez Biography." Alexandria Ocasio-Cortez, About. Accessed May 21, 2021. https://ocasio-cortez.house.gov/about/biography.

CHAPTER 4: VENUS

Basu, S., J. Jongerden, and G. Ruivenkamp. "Development of the drought tolerant variety Sahbhagi Dhan: exploring the concepts commons and community building." *International Journal of the Commons*, 11, no.1 (March 2017): 144–170. http://doi.org/10.18352/ijc.673.

Bollier, David. "The Commons as a Template for Transformation." Great Transition Initiative. April 2014. http://www.greattransition.org/publication/the-commons-as-a-template-for-transformation.

Davis, Krystle M. "20 Facts and Figures to Know When Marketing to Women," *Forbes*. May 13, 2019. https://www.forbes.com/sites/forbescontentmarketing/2019/05/13/20-facts-and-figures-to-know-when-marketing-to-women/.

Johnson, Karen., and A. H. Almaas. *The Power of Divine Eros: The Illuminating Force of Love in Everyday Life*. United States: Shambhala, 2013.

McGregor, Jean. "This Former Surgeon General Says There's a 'Loneliness Epidemic' and Work Is Partly to Blame." *Washington Post,* On Leadership. October 4, 2017. https://www.

washingtonpost.com/news/on-leadership/wp/2017/10/04/this-former-surgeon-general-says-theres-a-loneliness-epidemic-and-work-is-partly-to-blame/.

Murthy, Vivek. *Together.* New York: Harper Wave, 2020.

Nicole, Pierre, and Blaise Pascal. *Pensées de Pascal.* Paris: Firmin-Didot Frères, Fils, et Cie, 1877.

Simons, Nina. *Nature, Culture & the Sacred: A Woman Listens for Leadership.* Housatonic, MA: Green Fire Press, 2019. Kindle.

CHAPTER 5: MARS

Bainbridge-Cohen, Bonnie. "Yield Versus Collapse." *Body-Mind Centering.* Accessed May 16, 2021. https://www.bodymindcentering.com/yield-verse-collapse/.

Baver, Kristin. "8 Great Life Teachings from Yoda." Star Wars, Characters and Histories. June 17, 2017. https://www.starwars.com/news/8-great-life-teachings-from-yoda.

brown, adrienne maree. *Holding Change: The Way of Emergent Strategy Facilitation and Mediation.* Chico, CA: AK Press, 2021.

Lad, Vasant. "Ayurveda: A Brief Introduction and Guide." The Ayurvedic Institute. 2006. Accessed June 24, 2021. https://www.ayurveda.com/resources/articles/ayurveda-a-brief-introduction-and-guide.

Macy, Joanna. "The Great Turning." *Ecoliteracy* (blog), *Center for Ecoliteracy.* June 29, 2009. https://www.ecoliteracy.org/article/great-turning.

Macy, Joanna, and Molly Brown. "Practices." Work That Reconnects Network, Resources. Accessed June 26, 2021. https://workthatreconnects.org/resources/practices/.

CHAPTER 6: JUPITER

Blakeslee, Nate. *Tulia: Race, Cocaine, and Corruption in a Small Texas Town*. New York: PublicAffairs, 2006.

Congress.gov. "H.R.3794 — 116th Congress (2019–2020): Public Land Renewable Energy Development Act of 2019." December 18, 2020. https://www.congress.gov/bill/116th-congress/house-bill/3794.

Eisenstein, Charles. *Sacred Economics: Money, Gift, and Society in the Age of Transition*. United States: North Atlantic Books, 2011.

Evans, Andrew. "Alexander Graham Bell, Digital Nomad." *National Geographic*. June 22, 2011. https://www.nationalgeographic.com/travel/article/tweeting-place.

Frawley, David. "Planets in the Vedic Literature," *Indian Journal of History of Science* 29, no. 4 (July 18, 1994): 495–496, 502. https://insa.nic.in/writereaddata/UpLoadedFiles/IJHS/Vol29_4_1_DFrawley.pdf.

Global Footprint Network. "Ecological Footprint." Accessed May 18, 2021. https://www.footprintnetwork.org/our-work/ecological-footprint/.

Gupta, Vanita. "Hope Is a Discipline: Fighting for Justice in Perilous Times" (speech). March 6, 2018. In "Richman Distinguished Fellowship in Public Life," Past Fellows. Brandeis University. Transcript and video, 1:08:02. https://www.brandeis.edu/richmanfellow/recipients/past/gupta.html.

Hewitt, Damon. "Re: Support of Nomination of Vanita Gupta to Associate Attorney General at United States Department of Justice" (letter). Lawyers' Committee for Civil Rights Under Law to the United States Senate. March 8, 2021. https://lawyerscommittee.org/wp-content/uploads/2021/03/LC-Letter-of-Support_Gupta_DOJ-FINAL.pdf.

Leadership Conference on Civil and Human Rights. Accessed June 26, 2021. https://civilrights.org/.

National Geographic Magazine. "The Race Issue." April 2018. https://www.nationalgeographic.com/magazine/issue/april-2018.

Wallace, Chantelle. "National Geographic CEO Says Nonprofit's Mission is Bringing the World to Readers." University of Texas at Austin. McCombs School of Business. April 11, 2007. https://web.archive.org/web/20100528153618/http://www.mccombs.utexas.edu/news/pressreleases/fahey07.asp.

Wamsley, Laurel. "'National Geographic' Reckons with Its Past: 'For Decades, Our Coverage Was Racist.'" *National Public Radio*. The Two-Way. March 12, 2018. https://www.npr.org/sections/thetwo-way/2018/03/12/592982327/national-geographic-reckons-with-its-past-for-decades-our-coverage-was-racist/.

CHAPTER 7: SATURN

Bandele, Asha and Patrisse Cullors. *When They Call You a Terrorist: A Black Lives Matter Memoir*. New York: St. Martin's Publishing Group, 2018.

Biomimicry Institute. "Biomimicry: What Is Biomimicry?" Accessed May 19, 2021. https://biomimicry.org/what-is-biomimicry/.

Cockburn, Chloe. "Reimagine Safety: Money Can't Buy Criminal Justice Reform. But It Can Fuel a Movement." *The Washington Post*. March 16, 2021. https://www.washingtonpost.com/opinions/2021/03/16/los-angeles-criminal-justice-reform-money/.

Cullors, Patrisse. "Op-Ed: My Brother's Abuse in Jail Is a Reason I Co-founded Black Lives Matter. We Need Reform in L.A." *Los Angeles Times*. April 13, 2018.

https://www.latimes.com/opinion/op-ed/la-oe-cullors-los-angeles-sheriff-jail-reform-20180413-story.html.

Cullors, Patrisse. "Words Speak Immeasurable Truths." Author page. Accessed May 19, 2021. https://patrissecullors.com/author/.

Katie, Byron and Stephen Mitchell. *Loving What Is: Four Questions That Can Change Your Life*. New York: Three Rivers Press, 2003.

Kimmerer, Robin Wall. *Braiding Sweetgrass: Indigenous Wisdom, Scientific Knowledge, and the Teachings of Plants*. Minneapolis: Milkweed Editions, 2013.

Shiva, Vandana. "Everything I Need to Know I Learned in the Forest." *Yes! Magazine*. May 3, 2019. https://www.yesmagazine.org/issue/nature/2019/05/03/vandana-shiva-seed-saving-forest-biodiversity.

Stanton, Andrew, dir. *Finding Nemo*. 2003; Emeryville, CA: Pixar, 2013, DVD.

United Nations. "Greta Thunberg Tells World Leaders 'You Are Failing Us,' as Nations Announce Fresh Climate Action." Climate and Environment. September 23, 2019. https://news.un.org/en/story/2019/09/1047052.

CHAPTER 8: RAHU

Brock, Arthur. "Wealth: A Living Systems Model." ArtBrock. Accessed June 4, 2021. https://www.artbrock.com/metacurrency.

Foor, Daniel. "Animism and Earth Ritual." Ancestral Medicine. Accessed May 20, 2021. http://www.ancestralmedicine.org/animism.

Jacobs, Jane. *The Nature of Economies*. New York: Knopf Double-day Publishing Group, 2002.

Kempton, Sally. "Tantra in Everyday Practice." Aim Healthy U. Accessed June 29, 2021. https://www.aimhealthyu.com/courses/tantra-101-awaken-to-your-most-divine-life.

Nhat Hanh, Thich. "Please Call Me by My True Names" (poem). *The Mindfulness Bell*. Autumn 2004. Accessed June 25, 2021. https://www.mindfulnessbell.org/archive/2015/06/poem-please-call-me-by-my-true-names.

Saotome, Mitsugi. *The Principles of Aikido*. Boulder, CO: Shambhala, 1989.

Scott, Ridley, dir. *Blade Runner*. Burbank, CA: Warner Bros. Pictures, 1982.

Spiller, Jan. *Astrology for the Soul*. New York: Bantam Books, 1997.

Steiner, Achim. "The Next Frontier: Human Development and the Anthropocene (Foreword)" (PDF). Overview: Human Development Report 2020. United Nations Development Programme. Accessed December 16, 2020. http://hdr.undp.org/sites/default/files/hdr_2020_overview_english.pdf.

CHAPTER 9: KETU

Avritt, Julie Jordan, and Thomas Hübl. *Healing Collective Trauma: A Process for Integrating Our Intergenerational and Cultural Wounds*. Boulder, CO: Sounds True, 2020.

Calderon de la Barca, Laura. "Definition of Collective Trauma and What it takes to Heal It." Therapy for Mexico website. Accessed May 21, 2021. https://www.terapiaparamexico.com/english/collectivetrauma.html.

Carey, Benedict. "Can We Really Inherit Trauma?" *The New York Times*. Dec. 10, 2018. https://www.nytimes.com/2018/12/10/health/mind-epigenetics-genes.html.

Masters, Robert Augustus. *Spiritual Bypassing: When Spirituality Disconnects Us from What Really Matters*. Berkeley, CA: North Atlantic Books, 2010.

Teilhard de Chardin, Pierre. *The Phenomenon of Man*. New York: HarperCollins, 2008.

Tyson, Neil deGrasse. *Astrophysics for People in a Hurry*. New York: W. W. Norton & Company, 2017.

van der Kolk, Bessel A. *The Body Keeps the Score: Brain, Mind, and Body in the Healing of Trauma*. New York: Penguin Books, 2014.

van der Kolk, Bessel A. "The Body Keeps the Score: Memory and the Evolving Psychobiology of Posttraumatic Stress," *Harvard Review of Psychiatry* vol. 1, no. 5 (January 1994): 253–265. doi: 10.3109/10673229409017088.

CHAPTER 10: FATE AND FREE WILL

Deans, Carrie, and Keith Maggert. National Center for Biotechnical Information. "What Do You Mean, "Epigenetic"?" *Genetics* 199, no. 4 (April 2015): 887–896. https://doi.org/10.1534/genetics.114.173492.

Feuerstein, Georg. "200 Key Sanskrit Yoga Terms." *Yoga Journal*. August 28, 2007. https://www.yogajournal.com/yoga-101/200-key-sanskrit-yoga-terms/.

Forrest, Steven. *The Inner Sky*. Borrego Springs: Seven Paws Press, Inc. 2012. Kindle.

Hübl, Thomas. *Healing Collective Trauma: A Process for Integrating Our Intergenerational and Cultural Wounds.* Boulder, CO: Sounds True, 2020. p. 32.

Kelleher, James. *Path of Light: Introduction to Vedic Astrology.* Volume I. San Francisco: Ahimsa Press, 2006.

Kempton, Sally. *Awakening Shakti.* United States: Sounds True, 2013.

Tolkien, J. R. R. *The Fellowship of the Ring. The Lord of the Rings,* Book 1. New York: HarperCollins Publishers, 2009.

Yehuda, Rachel, and Amy Lehrner. "Intergenerational Transmission of Trauma Effects: Putative Role of Epigenetic Mechanisms." *World Psychiatry* 17, no. 4 (October 2018): 243–257.8. https://doi.org/10.1002/wps.20568.

CHAPTER 11: HOW TO BE AN AGENT OF EVOLUTION

Arroyo, Stephen. *Astrology, Karma & Transformation: The Inner Dimensions of the Birth Chart.* Sebastopol, CA: CRCS Publications, 2011

Baker, Richard, Huston Smith, and Shunryu Suzuki. *Zen Mind, Beginner's Mind.* Boulder: Shambhala Publications, 2006.

Calvino, Italo. *If on a Winter's Night a Traveler.* Boston: HMH Books, 2012.

Kelleher, James. *Path of Light: Introduction to Vedic Astrology.* Volume I. San Francisco: Ahimsa Press, 2006.

Wilder, Thornton. *The Bridge of San Luis Rey: A Novel.* New York: Harper Perennial, 2014.

ACKNOWLEDGMENTS

———

It takes a village to raise an author. I give thanks to the village who raised me.

First and foremost, I thank my clients. I am supremely blessed by the trust you place in me when we enter sacred space, explore your chart, your life, your dreams, and your evolutionary edge. I am so fortunate to get to do this mystical work with you. Spending time with you in session over the years has taught me the concepts presented in this book.

I am deeply grateful to the Agents of Evolution who join me in these pages, offering their stories and insights, and for serving as real-world archetypes we can look to for inspiration. Gratitude also to these Agents of Evolution for sharing their stories with me, even though they do not appear in the book: Aditi Goswami, Sepi Hakimzadeh, Monica Silva-Gutierrez, Jeanine Moy, and Chris Hardy.

Big ups to my outstanding editors, Jessica Fleischman and Katie Sigler, for shaping the content and making it sing!

Pranams to my advance readers for their wisdom, insights, and input on the content and its presentation: Lila Galindo, Katie Teague, Bill Gholson, Mohini Kane, Magalí Morales, and James Kelleher.

Heartfelt thank yous to these bright beings:

Meera Laube Szapiro, for sisterhood and 24/7 love and support.

Mohini and Bernie Kane, for housing me while I was "pregnant" with this book, and to Mo for being the most gracious book doula a Soul could ask for.

Catherine Parrish, for mentorship and for modeling what it means to be an Agent of Evolution.

Katie Teague, for friendship, photos, coaching, checking all my baldashery, and for help understanding and articulating complex concepts.

Laura Loescher, for friendship, guidance, inspiration, food, poems, and beauty that kept me going throughout the process of writing this book.

Duane and Coleen Elgin, for mentorship, training, collaboration, solidarity, and friendship. And for their important life's work, The Choosing Earth Project.

Karen Williams, for friendship and for help workshopping the concepts in the Agents of Evolution class series.

Margaret Brownlie, for enduring friendship, memorable equinox and solstice magic, and tangible support.

Kris Martin, for geeking out with me over wisdom traditions and for tangible support.

Padma Gordon, the older sister I always wanted, for showing me around the book publishing world.

Kimberley Healey, for damn productive weekly writing sessions.

Steve Davidson, for encouragement and pre-sale campaign mojo.

Asha Mclaughlin, for following the Shakti with me and forgiving my irritability during book deadlines.

Lisa Abbott, Angela Zusman, sadhana sisters, for their maha support.

Elizabeth Topp, for enduring friendship and support.

Praise to my ancestors!

Special gratitude to my mother, Elizabeth Chempolil-Laube; and my father and step-mother, Gottfried Laube and Liz Watkins. Your Love is everything to me.

And thanks to Miriam, Rex, Meera, Avi, Moni, Ashley, Braedyn, Garrett, Eliani, Angela (and all the little ones yet to come!)—my dear family—your Love lights up my world.

Thanks a million, Eric Koester, Brian Bies, and my amazing publishing team at New Degree Press!

Eternal gratitude to my teachers in this lifetime: my root guru—whose teachings on the nakshatras in a courtyard in India lit the flame, Adyashanti, James Kelleher, Ram Butler, Sally Kempton, Thomas Hübl, Byron Katie, David Elliott, and Owl.

A huge, rousing chorus of thank-you's to the book's pre-sale campaign supporters!

Without you, this book would not have made it to press:

Meera Laube
Elizabeth Laube
Avi Szapiro
Lynne & Ralph Rosa
Angie Farynnyk
Moni & Ashley Laube
Bahara Stapelberg
Laura Loescher
Mandy Roberts
Andrea & David Kinsley
Jana Holm & Howie Schechter
Coleen LeDrew Elgin & Duane Elgin
Jane & Jimmy Baldwin
Heather Ambler
Katie Teague
Ann Hempelmann
Rosemary Robinson
Nala Cardillo
Karen Williams
James Jarvis
Margaret Brownlie
Lisa Wideman
Jacki Strenio
Kate Quarfordt
Angela Zusman

Kathryn Toth
Bethany & Ronnie Mutone
Lauren Kliminchenko
Catherine & Bill Parrish
Steve Davidson
Ginny Auer
Sarah Emerson
Asha & Mark Mclaughlin
Kristine Martin
Laurie Ferreira
Kristoffer Nelson
Kristine Pandey
Lisa Abbott
Nina Simons
Mildred Ruiz-Sapp
Hanna Levinson
BJ Garcia
Lucy Meckler
Lucia Kastner
Elisabeth Mohlmann
Megan Dixon
Misty Muñoz
Lauren Krasnodembski
Eric Koester
Miriam Laube & Rex Young
Nikki Costello
Shari Fox

Sharon Kraus
Kathleen Kook
Kimberley Healey
Kristina Wingeier
Jen Jones
Sarah Shaw
Joanne Feinberg
Dune Thomas

Stefania Masoni
Anamaria Ayala
Charles Hillary
Lila Galindo
Rita Baldo
Robin Stiehm
Greta Muscat Azzopardi
Suni Sanchez